Still Standing

Holding On To Hope, Despite Life's Storms

Ayesha A. Thomas

MaH®

Milk and Hunee Success Education, LLC

Milk and Hunee Success Education, LLC

Ayesha A. Thomas 2016©

All rights reserved. No part of this book may be reproduced in print, or by photostatic means, or in any other manner without the express permission of the author and publisher.

Table of Contents

Forewords 1

City Girl Turned Country 4

Transition/Searching 13

A Mother's Love 21

Looking for love 27

Awakening 32

Gideon Experience 65

Overcomer/Restorer 69

Grace and Mercy 73

He That is Without Sin 77

God of a Second Chance 83

Our Big Day 88

Dedication 92

ACKNOWLEDGEMENTS 94

Forewords

The author has been a fighter from birth; the odds were against her. Both parents used drugs at a significantly early age. Her father was caught up in a situation that eventually landed him in prison for life. Being born out of wedlock, you will find that the author was left with the devices and instability of a mother and drug user who moved from place to place, leaving no sentiments of a good home to raise her daughter. This led to relatives stepping in and moving the author from the inner city to a country town in Georgia. Although she had a stable life, generational curses eventually caught up to her, not in the way of drugs, but having children out of wedlock. She faced the struggles of marriage and eventually adversity took over and led to a divorce and becoming a single mother. Throughout the challenges of life, she knew of God but when she finally let go and surrendered her life to him, is when the relationship with the lord established a stand and a will to fight, despite the circumstances.

As Christians, we find it difficult to stand on faith. There must be a belief that God will supply all our needs no matter what defies us. Psalm 28-7 "The lord is my strength and my shield, my heart trusts in him and he helps me ". This book will encourage the reader to not settle for setbacks, but instead stand and fight so that your circumstances will change for the good, living a life of victory instead of disgrace and uncertainty.

As you read this book you will find that challenges are just a test of time. It takes a person through the will of God that will stand up and say that's enough and know that God is with them. The author is a personal witness to what can go wrong in life and therefore surrendering to God has established the confidence and determination to prosper. Proverbs 16-20, "Those who give heed to instructions prosper, and blessed are those who trust in the lord." The author has surrendered her life to God and by doing so her will to fight increased and her circumstances changed. Her words will give others hope and a desire to work towards a better tomorrow by trusting in the lord.

Derek Thomas, husband

Ayesha has been and continues to be one the most beautiful, genuine people that I have met. As a matter of fact, we met not knowing that we would have a bond that would carry on for years to come. I was checking into the hospital to have an outpatient procedure done and she was the one that registered me. Fast forward a few months later and I saw her again at church. We instantly remembered each other as we recalled our first meeting and we began talking about each other's hair styles. What Ayesha didn't know was that I was in a broken place in my life and I prayed that God would bring me the right kind of friends and I knew that she was a keeper, the friend that I had been praying for. As we began to know more about each other, it was her story of triumph that blew me away. I learned that both her mom and dad, though now passed on, were addicted to drugs, which left her to be raised by her aunt and grandfather. I had the opportunity to learn and hear of so many of the oppositions that she was faced with. One would never think that this beautiful, vivacious woman would have experienced some of the horrible things that she has. As you read this book I pray that you are inspired to keep it moving no matter what twists and turns life bring about… there is hope if you do not give up.

LaTasha Davis, friend

Chapter 1

City Girl Turned Country

"For I Know the plans that I have for you declares the Lord, plans to prosper you and not to harm you, plans to give you a future and hope"

Jeremiah 29:11

I was born Ayesha Aqueelah Bradshaw in Newark New, Jersey on May 22, 1976, at Beth Israel Hospital, to Reginald Beckwith and Wendy Bradshaw. Although they never married, I believe that they both loved one another deeply. I say this because of the respect that they had for each other. No matter who my father or mother dated, they would always seem to come back together. I am the only child, although after talking to my dad, he confided in me regarding a young lady of his past. He told me that he was possibly the father of the child she was carrying. However, due to the circumstances of her being young and her faith as a Jehovah's Witness, as well as her parents' religious belief, they preferred that she take other measures regarding the child's welfare by putting the baby up for adoption. The family wanted to try and prevent shame for their family. Technically, if my father is identified as the father of this child, then there is a chance that I may have a sibling somewhere in this world. Growing up as an only child, I always wished for another sibling, but I would have preferred to be in the same home growing up with them. At 18 years of age my mother gave birth to me. She had dreams of marrying and living what most call, "the American dream." Unfortunately, she found herself in the same situation as most teenagers growing up in Newark, in the inner city of economic depression, where drugs, alcohol, and sex was the downfall of many. Being an only child, my mother and I would spend much time together talking. My mom would share stories about how she would take care of her mother when she would come home from pulling double shifts, to ensure food was on the table and clothes was provided for her younger siblings, and that she would be so tired. Mom said that Grandma's feet used to swell from standing on them all day and so when she would get off work and come home, my mom would massage them for her. My mom told me that she used to cook and clean the house and watch after all of her younger siblings before her mother passed away. I was two months old when my grandma died of ovarian cancer. My mom felt all alone. Mainly because all of the siblings that she once helped care for were all scattered from Jersey to Ga. My mom was the only younger sibling that was too old to receive a social security check. Therefore, it is my assumption, and I say this with the utmost respect, that because she was not able to bring in any money, she was possibly deemed a reject by some of those that may have otherwise taken her in. Therefore, she mainly ended up alone, well not quite alone, because she did have me (smile). I am reminded briefly of the scripture that reads, "when my mother and father forsake me, and then the Lord will take me up." You see, my mom was left alone, but through it all, wrong choices, blunders, and lessons learned, the heavenly father had not forsaken her. It was the grace of God that kept her all of the thirty-nine years that she walked this earth.

After my mother lost her mom, she then turned to my father's mother, whom everyone calls Nana. I do not remember either of my grandparents growing up, although I did have a vision once, in which I described to an aunt and uncle of mine, the way my grandmother's room looked. They both laughed at me and said that what I described was a basic room, but I know the vision that I had. Anyways, my mother and my paternal grandma, Nana, started to bond more, but then suddenly Nanna passed away, and now my mom was all alone again. My father was not stable like he should have been during this time and eventually mom turned to the streets and drugs. I was a baby, so I do not remember much other than, having to stay with different relatives in New Jersey. I knew that I had a huge family, and they were all very supportive of me. I was with some of my favorite cousins and aunts in New Jersey. One of my aunts, who always made me laugh was Louise Douglas. Louise was hilarious, and she was quite the character, so to speak. I use to love going over to Aunt Louise's house because this is where everyone in the family, as well as everyone not in the family, hung out. I remember her husband, Uncle Archie always teasing me with his pocket knife, saying that he was going to cut off my ear. He was so funny. On Fridays, Uncle Archie and Aunt Louise would take me to this burger place that was popular back then, called Roy Rogers. I was always excited to go to Roy Rogers and get a juicy burger. Now they have both passed away, and I miss them.

My mom and dad would date on and off. It was almost as if they could not stay away from one another long. I remember my father renting a room from an elderly lady so that my mom and I could have somewhere safe to sleep. Everything was going well, until my dad's drug habit rehashed. Dad started stealing from the lady. Well, she put us all out in the cold, and we had to find somewhere to stay. Dad pretty much burned bridges with almost all of his family, although he still had brothers and sisters that were willing to help him. I remember my dad and all his of his brothers looking alike to me as a child. Dad's oldest brother, next to oldest brother and one of his sisters looked like they were all white. The reason I describe them as looking white is mainly because their complexion was much lighter than anyone else and their hair was very fine and curly, which is what one mainly saw in the Caucasian family. My uncle Gerald and my dad look more alike to me than the others. My uncle Gerald reminds me so much of my father. He sounds like him and even calls my name just like my dad did.

I remember my mom attending the Essex Community College, which was downtown Newark and I attended the daycare right across the street. I do not remember a lot about the daycare other than we used to sleep on these hard blue cots. My mother tried hard to do something better with her life, but the streets kept calling her. After my mom and dad had decided to break up, mom started dating this guy named Al. Al was very nice at times, but he also had a terrible anger problem. Al would supply mom with drugs and so she became hooked on him instantly. We lived with Al for some time, until the family came and took me away. I remember jumping double dutch outside in the middle of the street one day with some friends in front of where we lived with Al, and I looked down the street and saw my father coming. I was so happy to see him that I started yelling "daddy, daddy, daddy" until he got closer. My dad gave me a hug, although he was walking fast as to be in a hurry. I was still happy to see him and see the smile on his face, which would always make my day. He would smile at me and I would smile back. I miss and love him so much. My dad continued to walk towards the house, and he said," Ayesha I am going upstairs to see Wendy, and I will be right back down." Even as a young child, something inside of me knew that this was not going to go well. The next thing I knew is my dad was running back down the stairs with his shirt open bleeding from his chest. Al had cut my father, when he had made an attempt to get my mother and I to leave with him. I remember asking my dad where he was going. He said, "Baby, I got to go." I was so sad, and I remember crying nonstop. I went to check on my mother, and she and Al had been fighting. It seemed that every man that my mom met, she had to fight. She was in many, many abusive relationships. My mom was looking for love in all the wrong places. What she did not realize at the time, is that the void that she felt, only the heavenly father could fill. Mom and I both suffered from the spirit of rejection. Mom really wanted to be loved, like many of us and I was wanting to have my mother in my life without fear of losing her to the streets.

It was not long before Al ended up moving mom and I to Alabama to his parents' house. We lived in Alabama for at least a year and Al beat my mom almost every weekend. I was a nervous wreck. I hated that my mom was in these abusive relationships, but I never wanted to leave her side. I always felt like if I stuck around that, maybe, just maybe, they would not hurt her too badly. I was wrong. Al beat my mother profusely. The last time he beat her, we ran across the street to a neighbor's house, and my mom called her brother in Georgia, my uncle Melvin. Uncle Melvin drove to Alabama and picked the two of us up and took us to Georgia. I was so happy that he came and got us, and I felt safe.

We lived in Georgia for a little while then mom met someone there and we moved to Florida for a little while. Well, it was not long before we ended up back in Georgia because mom was still using and the guy she dated beat her and was an alcoholic. It was during this time that my grandfather in Georgia, Floyzell Holloway, said enough was enough and he demanded that my mother bring me to Georgia, once and for all to live with him and my Aunt Bert. I moved in with them, but I did not like it at first. I was missing my mom like crazy, and I did not think they understood what I was going through. It was almost as if I was supposed just to be thankful that I had a stable roof over my head. Well, thankful I was, but as a child that had gone through and seen so much, I should have had counseling or some therapy. Nobody ever sought this out for me, or at least not to my knowledge. I guess back then people just took you in and that was it. I will say, given the knowledge and education that I currently have as a social work major, it is wise to seek help for any child or children that may have witnessed any abuse or have gone through any of the things that I went through. When this is not dealt with early in a child's life, the child or children could have many problems. Some of these issues are things such as constant fear, feeling rejection, mental disorders, depression, low self-esteem and possibly even other mental and emotional stress disorders.

"Weeping may endure for a night, but joy comes in the morning."

-Psalm 30:5

Chapter 2

Transition/Searching

During the entire time that I lived with my aunt and grandfather, I felt out of place. It had nothing to do with them; it was mainly because I was missing my mother and when all of my other cousins would be with their mothers I was not. I had several cousins and aunts that tried many times to be sure that I had as close to a normal life as possible. One of my cousins who I called Aunt Dona, was always the one that would defend me if someone talked bad about me or my mom. Dona pretty much did not play nobody trying to harm her family. She also use to buy me things and I even moved in with her for a short time. Then there was my aunt Willie Mae (Snook). I lived with aunt snook who is by the way my grandmother's sister, for a little while as well. My cousin Laura was there for me when I needed someone to talk to. Then there was my cousin Eleanor, she would help me with things that I needed growing up as well, although she and her family was military, whenever she was in Georgia, she took care of me. My two aunts that lived in Jersey, Rosemary and Christine, my mom sisters would send for me every summer as well and before sending me back to GA, they would take me school shopping. So as one can conclude, I had a lot of people in my life that tried to do the best they could with helping me all while trying to take care of their own families. However, as a child, all I could think about was being with my mother and living a normal life.

There were many lessons I had to learn by living in my grandfather's house. I learned how to cook and clean. I had to rake the grass every Saturday morning during the fall and winter months, and I also learned how to shell butter beans. I enjoyed shelling butter beans at first, but then it became dreadful. Granddad had several gardens and during the summer months, he would get up around five in the morning and would come back around noon with several buckets of butter beans for me to shell. If I had plans for the weekend, well let's just say it did not happen. My priority was to shell those beans and go nowhere. There were times when friends would stop by to see if I could get out of the house and then my grandfather would give them a bowl to shell beans as well. One would think that after all of the years of shelling butter beans that I would not want to see another bean in my life. Needless to say, butter beans and peas are two of my favorite vegetables, so I guess that form of discipline did not torment me too bad. Although my aunt Bert was so mean and fussed at me all the time, she tried to give me just about anything that I wanted. There were times that I would say, I would rather her give me a beating than to fuss at me. It did not take long for me to meet new friends living in Georgia. I had lots of friends, or let's just say people that I considered as friends. I think I had many best friends, too many to name (smile). I had a few young ladies that I ran with but to be honest, I never liked cliques. Even now that I am older, I still don't care to be a part of a clique. I like talking to any and everybody; I do not discriminate. It did not matter to me then if you were rich, poor, black or blue. Today, it still does not matter. Status does not matter to me. It never has and it never will. I enjoyed being with those that were cast out by others, or who were rejected by the majority. Maybe they did not have nice clean clothes, clean homes or even hair perms. I remember giving away clothes to them or washing their hair just to make them feel a little better. It is funny because, even now when I think back on these times, it seems I was already operating in my calling to serve and encourage others and give them hope, but unknowingly at the time. I just felt compelled to do these things even then. I never liked injustice or people mistreating others. So, you see, I would have never fit the status quo when I was younger, nor do I fit it now that I am older. I recall having a dream once, and in this dream it was a man that appeared and said to me "come on", but I kept saying, "I am not ready yet." I realize today that, this was my first encounter with the highest, Jehovah God. He was calling me to surrender then. However, I never actually shared this dream because I did not quite understand it like I do today. Needless to say, I started searching for this God, who was obviously interested in me. Although my aunt and grandfather made sure that I attended church and participated in the choir and youth ministries, I did not have a relationship with God. What I had was religion and I say religion because as long as I went to church and sang in the choir, I could live the remainder of my time as I wanted. That is what religion teaches right? I always knew there had to be more, so I started inviting the Jehovah's Witnesses, the Mormons and just about anybody else who may have had an answer or could help me discover that what was burning in me. I remember one morning when I was about to have study time in the living room with the Jehovah's Witnesses, they asked me if I knew who lived next door. I told them yes, that there was an elderly lady but she lived alone. They said we knocked and knocked on the door but nobody answered. I told them once we finished that I would go over and check on her. So after we studied and they went on their way, I decided to go next door and check on my elderly neighbor. When I knocked she still would not answer, so I went to the back and peeped through the window. I saw her laying on her bed, and I knew something was wrong. I went back to my house and to tell Granddad, and I also called 911. When they arrived, they called the police and kicked in her door. They discovered my neighbor, whose nickname was Red, had passed away while sleeping. She had swollen up a little, so they said that she had been in there a few days. Coincidentally, Red had two other older relatives that lived in the house before she moved there, that passed away in the house, and my grandfather discovered one and my aunt discovered the other. So basically, the three of us had discovered all three relatives deceased. As ironic as this may seem, after this, I had a dream about Red. I dreamed that she was telling me thank you for letting the police know she was in the house.

I graduated from Terrell Middle High School in Dawson, Georgia in May of 1995. One month before my graduation, I discovered I was pregnant with my first born. I was very scared and did not know what I was going to do, so I decided to write my aunt a letter a week before my graduation to let her know that I was pregnant. Boy was I nervous. I did not know what to expect, especially being that my aunt was known to be so mean at times. However, after she read it, she was very calm, which was totally opposite from what I had prepared myself for. My aunt told me that she was not happy about it, but that she would support me no matter what I decided to do. This made me feel better, but now my grandfather had to know. Sadly, I was not going to be the one to have to tell him this. My mother came to Georgia a few days before my graduation. My boyfriend at the time, and the father of my unborn child, drove me to Atlanta to pick my mother up from the airport. I was so happy to see her and I could not wait to tell her about me being pregnant. Once we were on the way back home from Atlanta, I told my mother that she was going to be a grandmother. Her initial reply was "stop playing E". She nicknamed me E, and still to this day, a lot of family and friends call me the same. I could tell that my mom was kind of excited, being that I am the only child and therefore, this would be her first grandchild.

My mother and I had moved into my first two bedroom, one and a half bath town home in Dawson. I was very excited. I remember telling my mom that I had been out looking for a place to move into before the baby was born. I knew that I was not going to live at my aunt and grandfather's house, not that they would not have wanted me to, but because I have always been a pioneer and a go-getter. I did not believe in waiting on anyone to do anything for me, if I was able to do it for myself. My first apartment was nice and simple, but it was mine. My mother's youngest brother had just relocated to GA after spending ten years in the Navy, he came to my rescue and purchased my very first living room set and dinette set with cash. I found my bedroom set in the Albany Herald and purchased it cash, with the exception of the mattresses. I purchased those separate. Things were looking pretty good for a young twenty-year-old mother. It was not long, that of course, my daughter's father moved in with me. We had our ups and downs like any other couple, but for the most part, things were okay, at least for a minute.

"If you can't fly, then run. If you cant run, then walk. If you cant walk, then crawl, but whatever you do, you have to keep moving forward."
                                        -Martin Luther King Jr.

Chapter 3

A Mother's Love

The morning of December 19, 1995. I woke up in pain. I had not slept well at all the night before. My cousin Kesha from Atlanta was at my house, and I told her to get my mom because I was hurting pretty bad. My mom was working with the property manager of the apartments, cleaning the apartments whenever tenants moved out. My mom came running asking, "is it time? Is it time?" I told my mom yes, I thought it was time, and so my mom, Kesha and myself loaded up in my 1989 Plymouth Sundance and headed to Albany. I could not reach my daughters father right away, but once to the hospital, he was already there. My uncle Melvin was already there as well. For some reason, they both had managed to beat us to the hospital. Wait a minute, I just remembered, my mom was driving my car and she was blowing at semi-trucks and telling them to get out of the way and just acting a bit nervous if you ask me. I finally told her to pull the car over and let me drive the rest of the way. So that is what I did. I drove myself along with mom and Kesha to the hospital, and this was the reason for the delay. The doctor came to check me and said that he was going to break my water and that the baby would be here shortly after that. For some reason, after hearing him say this, I began to feel nervous and scared all at the same time. I did not know what to expect. I was young and had never thought in a million years that I would have a child so soon. However, I gave birth to my daughter that night, and she weighed 7pounds 6 ounces. I thought she was the cutest, chubbiest baby I had ever seen. I remember crying when I first saw her, because I just could not believe that this little life had just come out of me. I could not believe that I had a baby, and my life would change and never be the same. I stayed in the hospital only two days and came home on my daughter's father's birthday. I bonded with my little girl and then reality started to sink in. I realized that having a child is absolutely no joke…It was changing diapers, being up all night, buying pampers, milk, clothes, going to doctor appointments, etc. My life had changed within a short period. I never knew that I could love someone the way that I loved my firstborn child. I realized from that point on there would never be anything that I would not do for my child. It was not long before I would become pregnant again, with my second daughter. You see, as a young teenager transitioning into adulthood, there was a void that I felt only my boyfriend at that time could fill. I did not realize then, that the only one that could ever fill that void was Jesus himself. Oh, how he longed to have a moment with me, but I was too blind to see this. God himself will allow things to happen in our lives to get our attention and cause us to call upon him. He will sometimes allow that boy or girl to break our heart so that we will realize that they should never have been in that place of affection in the first place. "Oh what needless pain we bare, all because we do not carry EVERYTHING to GOD in PRAYER." My boyfriend and I had not yet made any commitments other than shacking up from time to time. We were both young, and of course since neither of us had accepted God into our lives for real nor did we have a relationship with God, surely we could not possibly know how to love one another authentically. I especially say this, knowing what I know now about Love. I chose to have a second child knowing how hard it was for me with the first child. I thought I was in love and that this was the reason to continue to make babies. Well, this is not the answer. I did not think about my life, or the effects of having children out of wedlock could have on me.

In January of 1998, my mom had gotten a call saying that her sister Penny was moving to GA, and she was so thrilled. We were out shopping, and she told me to hurry and take her home because her sister would be pulling in anytime now. My mom was overjoyed, mainly because she and her sister shared a bond that many close sister's share. Needless to say, after my aunt moved to GA, her and my mom spent all day every day together until my mom was admitted to the hospital shortly thereafter. My mom stayed in the hospital for eight days. (*Biblical meaning of the number 8 is new beginnings*) How coincidental. My mom was supposed to get out of the hospital that following Monday, but she passed away that Sunday, February 1, 1998, just three months before my second child was born. I was devastated, lost, confused, angry, torn and broken. I could not believe that my mother, the woman who I fought so hard for, who I wanted so much to change her life and have this beautiful life with, was no longer here with me. She would not see her second grandchild, nor would she see either of them graduate high school. I was so confused and needed answers. I sought counseling, thinking this would help ease my pain and fill the void that was within me, but once again, I was wrong. I still, at this point, did not recognize that the only person who could fill the void that was within me, was Jesus. The help that I sought with the counseling did nothing for me. I still felt empty. I will never forget the first time that I experienced hearing the Holy Spirit speak to me. I was cleaning up my living room and still grieving for my mother, and suddenly I heard a still small voice whisper to me, "Isaiah 40." At first, I was like okay, this is somewhere in the Bible but, of course, I had never read it, so I was not sure what it said. All I knew and felt at this point was that when I finally got a chance to sit down after cleaning, I would open my bible and go to Isaiah 40. I sat on my bed and opened my Bible quickly turning to this particular passage of scripture. What I read blew my mind and gave me comfort and peace like nothing else I had sought. The first part of this chapter (Isaiah 40) talks about how, "her warfare is accomplished, and she has received of the Lord hands double for all of her sins." I saw this, and the tears began to fall. I cried uncontrollably because it was at that moment, sitting in my bedroom alone, God himself was giving me confirmation that my mom was okay, and there was no need to worry over her passing or whether or not she was okay due to the life she had lived. I knew from that point on without a doubt that the father really does speak, and he knows and feels everything that we can feel or go through. He is a loving and caring God, *Hallelujah!*

O Magnify the Lord with me, and let us exalt his name together

-Psalm 34:3

Chapter 4

Looking for love

It was not long after my mother passed away that my boyfriend and daughters' father, Mike, asked me to marry him. Mike and I got married February 13, 1999. Our wedding was planned within a short period and we moved into our new home. Well, actually Mike had already purchased the home right before he asked me to marry him. The first part of our marriage was not bad, although we were immature concerning the sacredness of our vows, we were determined to stay together. We worked rotating hours, with one working in the daytime and the other working the evening hours. We were not spending enough quality time together due to both of our work schedules. At the beginning of our marriage, we both were still drinking and, at times, partying, but things get old and sometimes you just want a change. I believe that when a couple is planning to get married, there should be counseling, and the two of them should be on one accord as far as what they both desire out of the relationship. I just assumed that if I got married, that was it. I did not understand nor did Mike understand the vows that we had made were not only to one another but ultimately they were unto God. We stayed married a few years, and then, once again, it came to an end, because when God is not involved in, or better yet, is not the foundation in any relationship, it will not last. I was still chasing after something or someone who I thought could fill the void that my heavenly father wanted so bad to fill. As a young mother of two, I compromised a lot based on what, I believed at the time, was going to be something great. Mike and I both talked about how neither one of us had both our parents in the home growing up, so neither one of us wanted that for our children. Well, Mike had his mom but not his dad in the home. I on the other hand had neither. Nevertheless, when God is not the foundation of anything, to include marriage, it will not last. Although we had dated for a long time and felt that we were ready for marriage, neither one of us was ready. After a few years of trying to make things happen in our own strength, we decided that instead of continuously hurting one another, we were better off saying our goodbyes.

As an insert to those that may be single and contemplating getting married, seek God on the matter and allow him to be the foundation. Do not want something so bad that you're willing to compromise your happiness for a moment. If you will wait on the Lord and learn to fall in love with him in your singleness, I can assure you that when God sends your mate, you will know how to honor and love them unconditionally. To the ladies, you don't have to sleep with a man to prove your love to him, my mistake more than once. You don't have to dress and show all of your flesh to prove to him you love him. Men, you don't have to brag about how much money you have or lie to her about how much you love only her to get her to love you more. This is all fruitless and seeds that's sewn in the flesh will not last. It is very temporary, I mean think about this. If God himself is LOVE, how is it that a man or a woman who has no real authentic relationship with Christ can possibly know how to love. It is not possible, no matter how we look at it. If a man or woman will not be faithful to the one who created them, how is that we can expect them to be faithful to us. Let me be very candid for a moment, ladies that thing between your thighs is not the best, no matter how much you want to think this. Men that thing between your things is not the best. I had to go there because after being around many women in my young and old age, I have heard many conversations where women will feel that If I put this so and so on him, he will be mine. This is so sad, he will only get that so and so, then go to the next sister, especially if he has no relationship with God. There is no way that one will be convicted. Conviction draws us toward Christ.

Ok, back to my story, once I had gotten a divorce, I can honestly say that this is where my life began to change for the better, although it did not feel good at the time, it was working out for my good. I say this because I was not used to being without my husband during that time, but neither did I want to stay because of the both of us being broken. That's just what we were, two broken people that needed a perfect God to fix our brokenness. Now let me add this, I am not saying that if you start out wrong in a marriage that you can't get it right by turning and allowing God to be the foundation. This is something that neither my husband at the time nor myself sought. However, thank God for GRACE and MERCY, because there are marriages today that may not have started off with God, but they found him along the way, and now for this cause, their marriages are made whole and better. The moral of this story is, WE NEED JESUS FOR EVERYTHING!!!

My people are destroyed from a lack of knowledge. Because you have rejected knowledge, I also reject you as my priests; because you have ignored the law of your God, I also will ignore your children.

-Hosea 4:6

Chapter 5

Awakening

My divorce was finalized July 2002. I moved to Albany, GA into my two-bedroom apartment working only a part-time job at JC Penney and with hardly any money. I had to do what I had to do, and I was determined not to give up. I have always been a strong minded and strong willed person and deep down, I knew that everything was going to be okay. I had a very close friend named Sophia, that stood by me during one of the hardest times in my life. Sophia and I had been friends ever since we were around ten or eleven. We used to play in the projects together and visit each other's houses. Sophia dressed so nice and her hair was always so cute. To this very day, she is still "fly" when you see her. Sophia stood by my side throughout the first few years of my divorce. We had our ups and downs as any friendship, but for the most part, we knew that we cared for one another and respected one another. It is good to know that when you are down and out and going through that someone is there for you. I thank God for the relationships that he has blessed me with that were authentic. Times were very hard for me being a single parent and having to do it all on my own. There were times that I did not know where our next meal would come from, or how I was going to pay my rent or put gas in my car. I was only making about one hundred fifty dollars a week, if that much. I will never forget being so broke one day after dropping my girls off at school and I came home to lay out on my bedroom floor, praying and crying out to God for help. At this time, I still was not attending church like I should or pursuing an authentic relationship with God. I was a part-time Christian. However, many of us know that God is not looking for part-time Christians or lukewarm Christians. I cried out to God this day and told him that I did not know what my children were going to eat when they came home from school. After crying and praying for about an hour on the floor of my bedroom, I got up and for the first time, I can say I heard a still small voice say, "put on those pants." I was looking in my closet when I heard this, so I grabbed that particular pair of pants. When I started to get dressed, I put my hand in my pocket, and in that pocket was a crisp twenty dollar bill. I could not believe it. I cried again saying, "thank you Jesus, thank you for hearing my cry because now I can buy my children something to eat." "In my distress I called to the Lord; I cried to my God for help. From his temple he heard my voice; my cry came before him, into his ears".(Psalm 18:6) Nobody knew what I was going through, nobody knew the nights I cried and stayed up wondering where our next meal was going to come from; not even my children knew because they never missed a meal. God was always faithful, even when I was not. Of all of the family and friends I had, nobody knew. Sometimes God will cause a deaf ear to come on those who would usually help you or he will cause you not to be on their minds for his namesake. The father wants to be glorified in ALL things and not us glorifying another. He will allow this so that when he brings you out of these dark places, you will know that it was him and only him that brought you out. He does not want anyone else to try and get the credit for what he has done and is doing in your life. Recently I heard the Holy Spirit say, "For me to get the Glory and for you to tell the Story." This is a powerful statement, and it was fitting for my situation over thirteen years ago and still today. There are some things that the Father is going to do on your behalf, that many will know that it was nobody but the Lord who was on your side that allowed these great things to take place in your life. He will be glorified in it all, but you will be his mouthpiece to testify of the goodness of the Lord.

There is a scripture in the book of James 1 that says,

Consider it pure joy my brothers and sisters, whenever you face trials of many kinds, knowing that the testing of your faith produces patience. But let patience have its perfect work, that you may be perfect and complete, lacking nothing. In other words, it is a blessing and a joyful thing to go through the hurt and the pain, because during these times is when your faith will grow. If you don't go through nothing, how in the world will you be of any help to anyone else. You see it's hard for me to listen to advice from people that have never gone through. I really be thinking, how is it they can tell me how to get through this and they never had to go through nothing. I am not saying that they may not be a little educated and tell me things based on their education, but when you have lived in poverty and God has brought you out!!(*Praise Break*) Or when you lost your momma and you though all hope was lost, but God brought you through it and you tell others about it. I think you get my drift now. I believe this is the main reason that we go through things, so that we can help someone else. I believe that the untold story, is the worse story because it is not helping anyone.

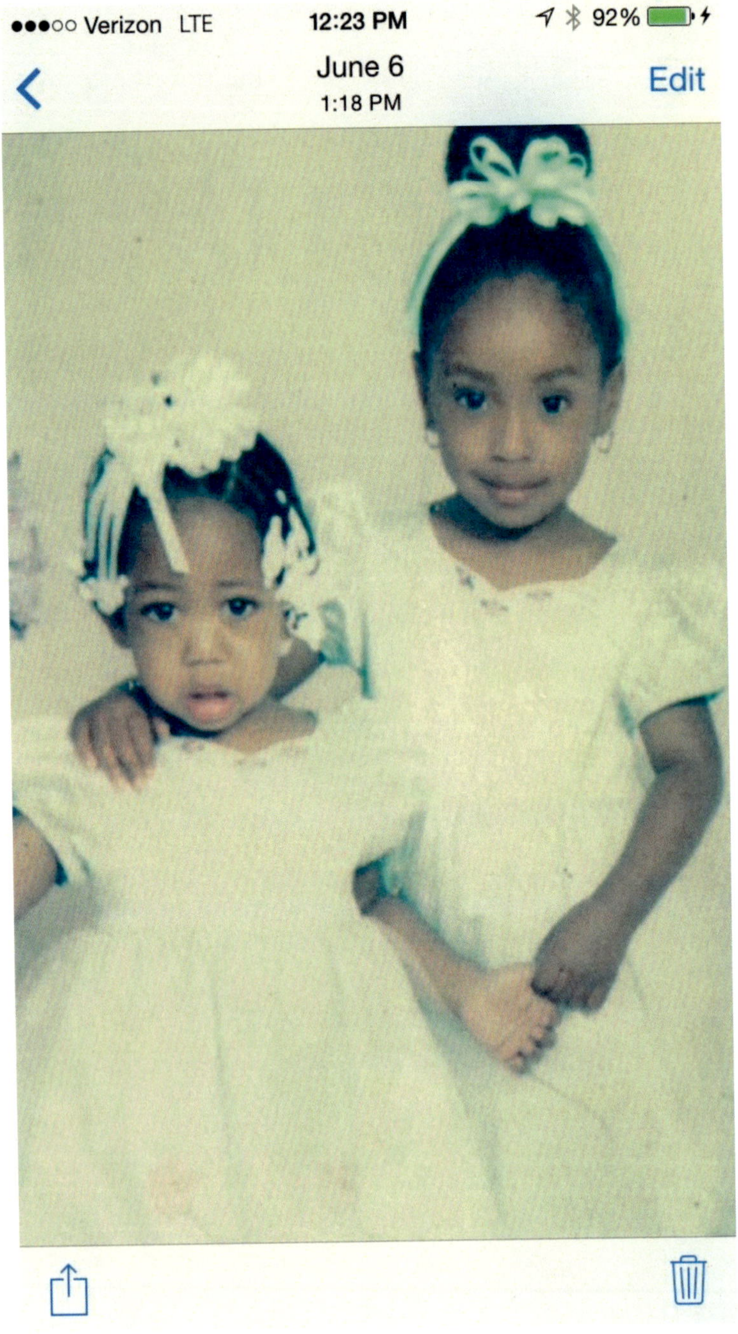
●●●○○ Verizon LTE
12:23 PM
92%
June 6
1:18 PM
Edit

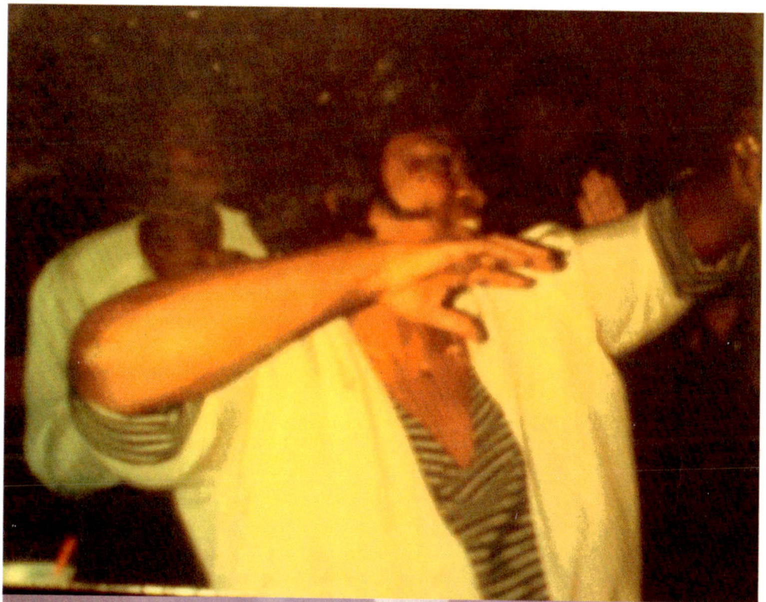

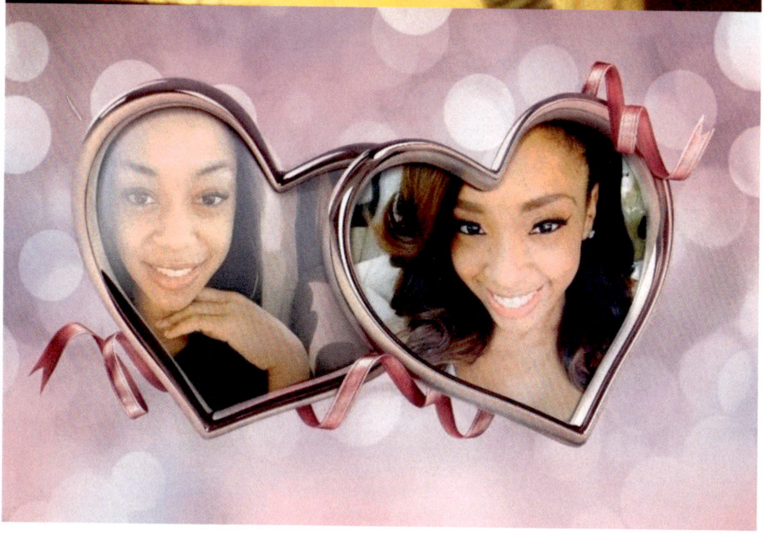

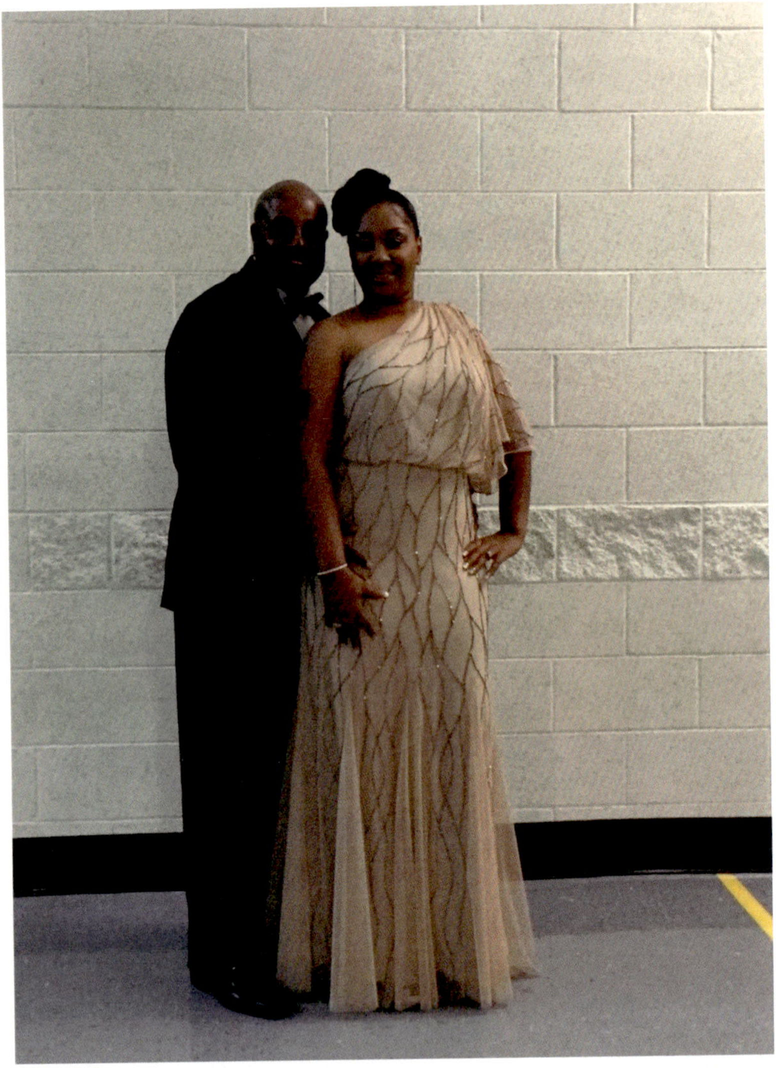

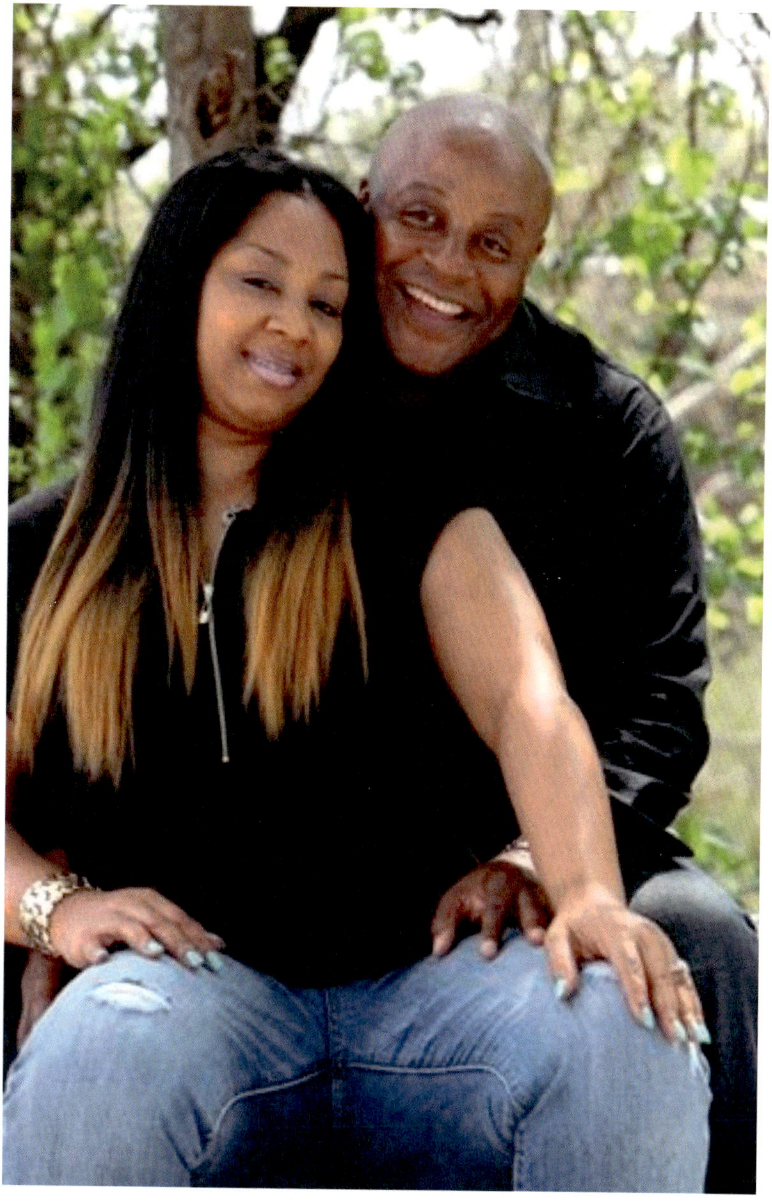

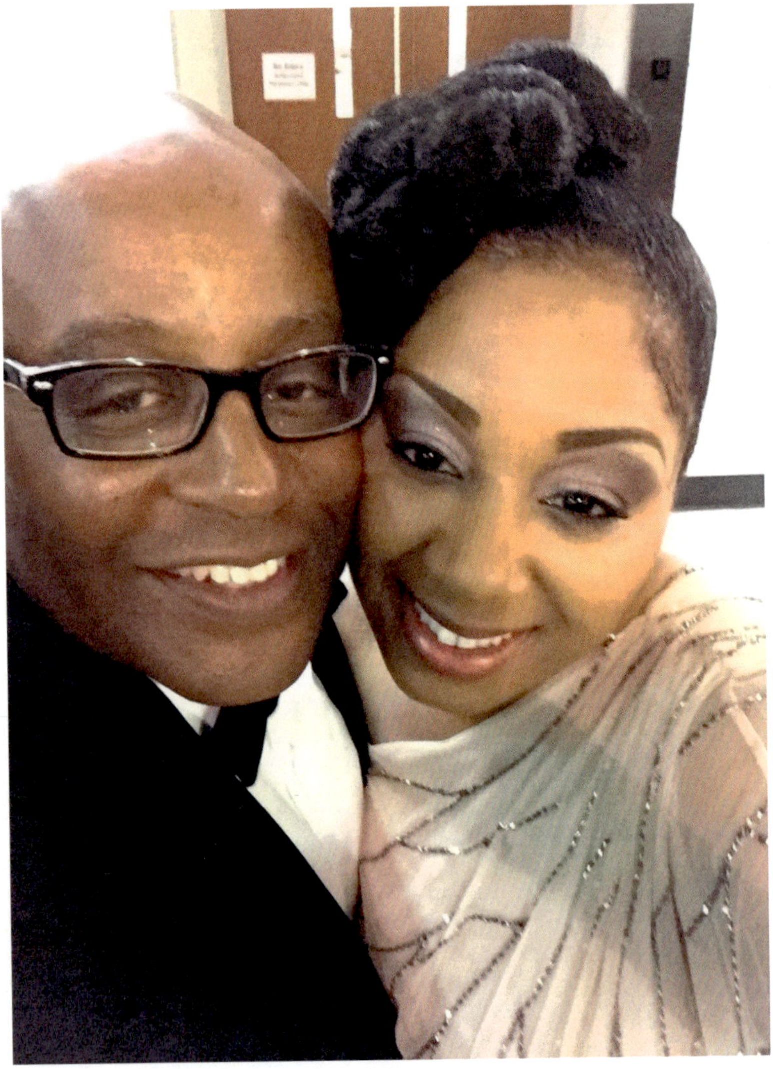

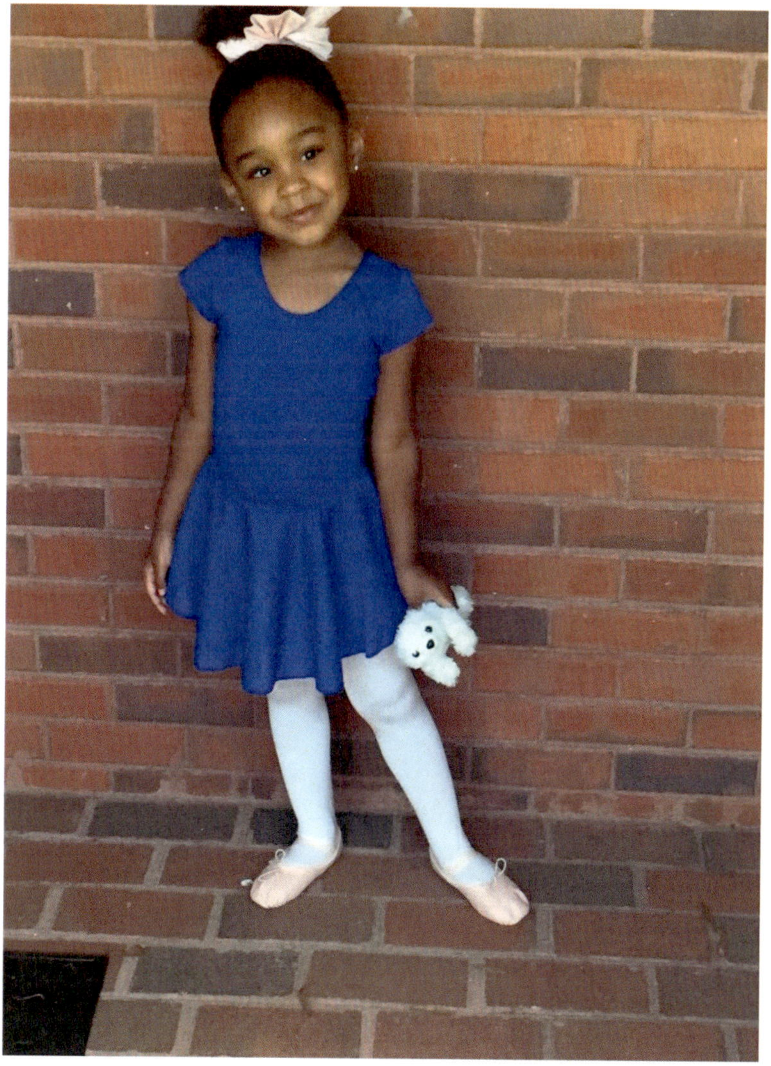

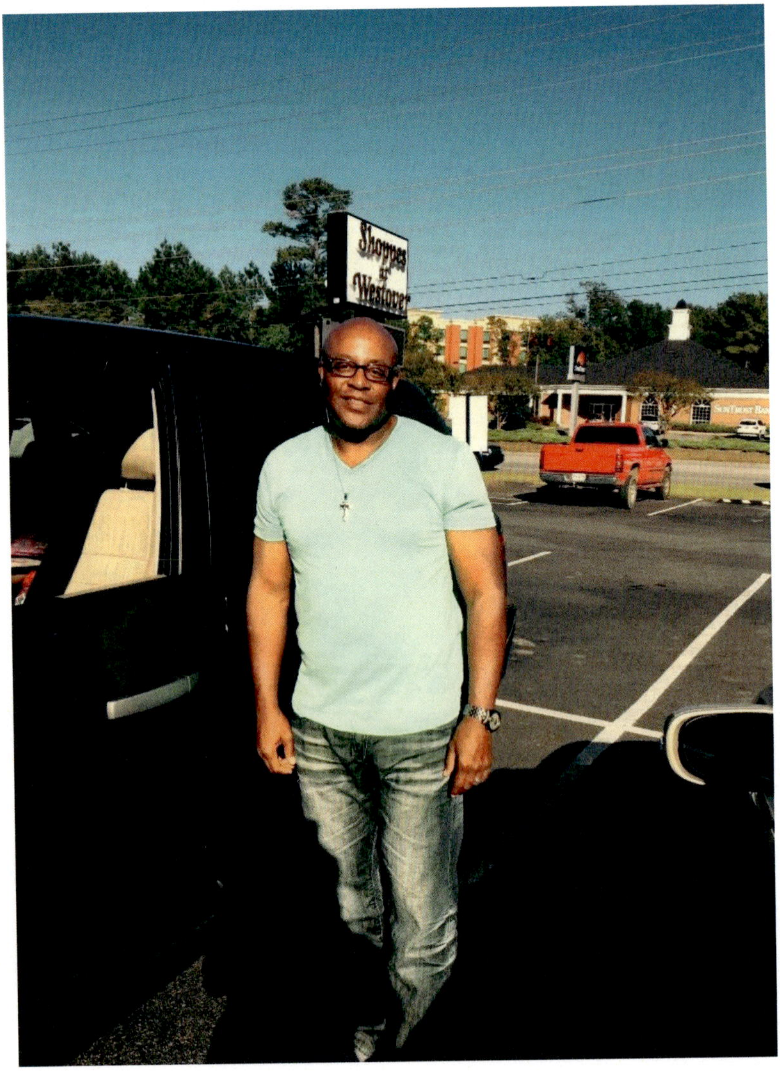
Shoppes
at
Westover

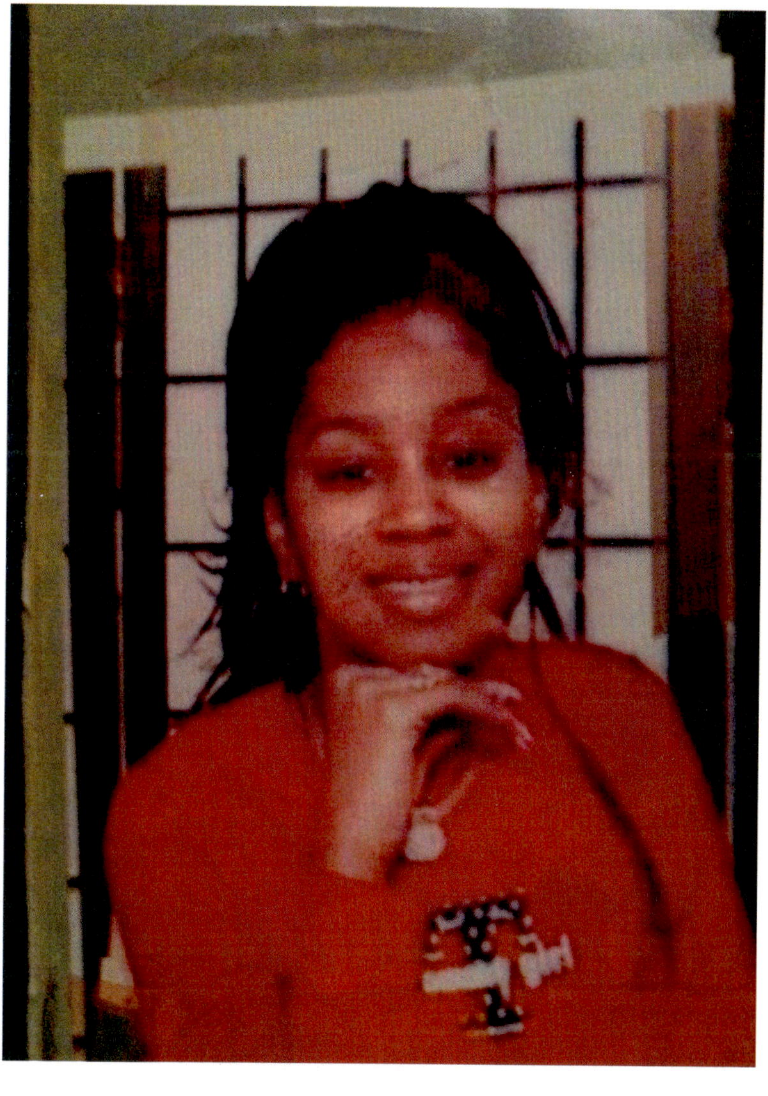

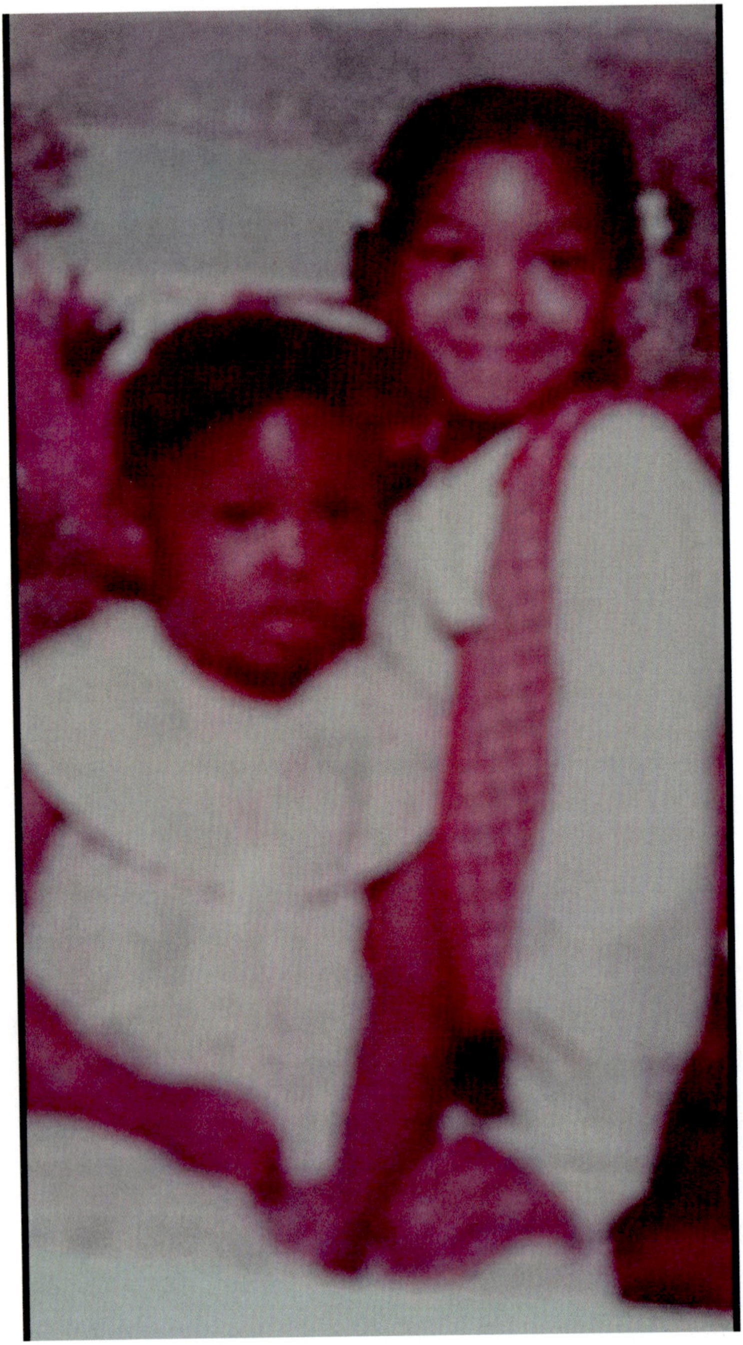

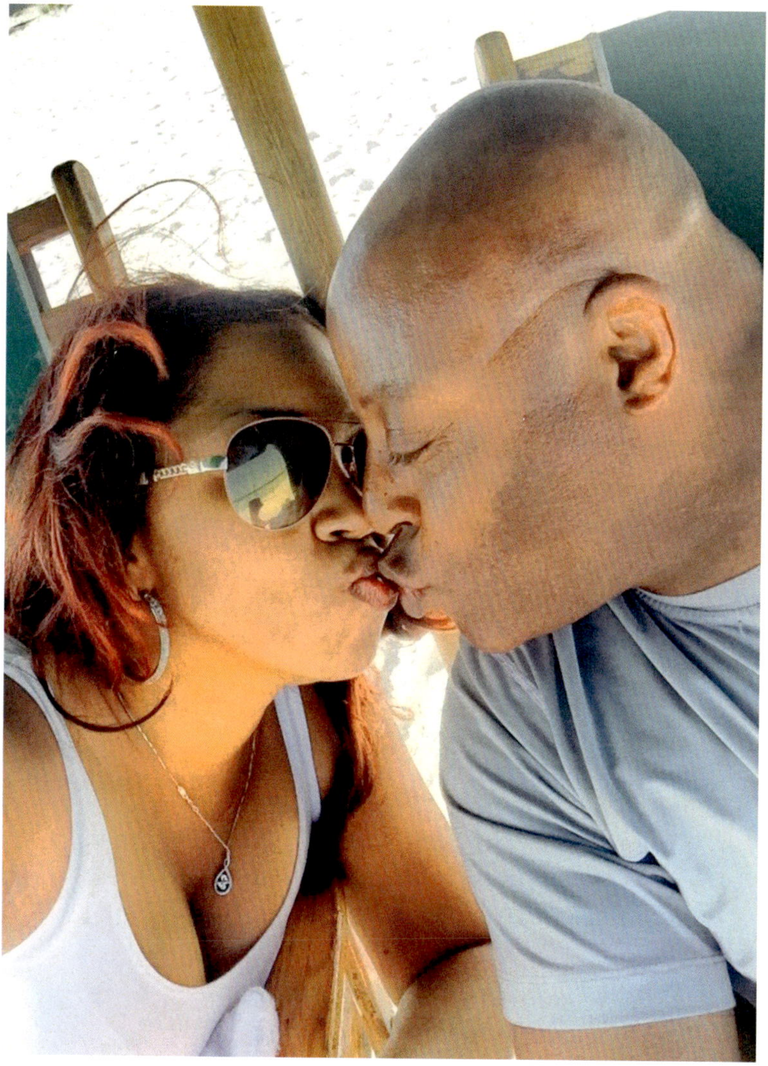

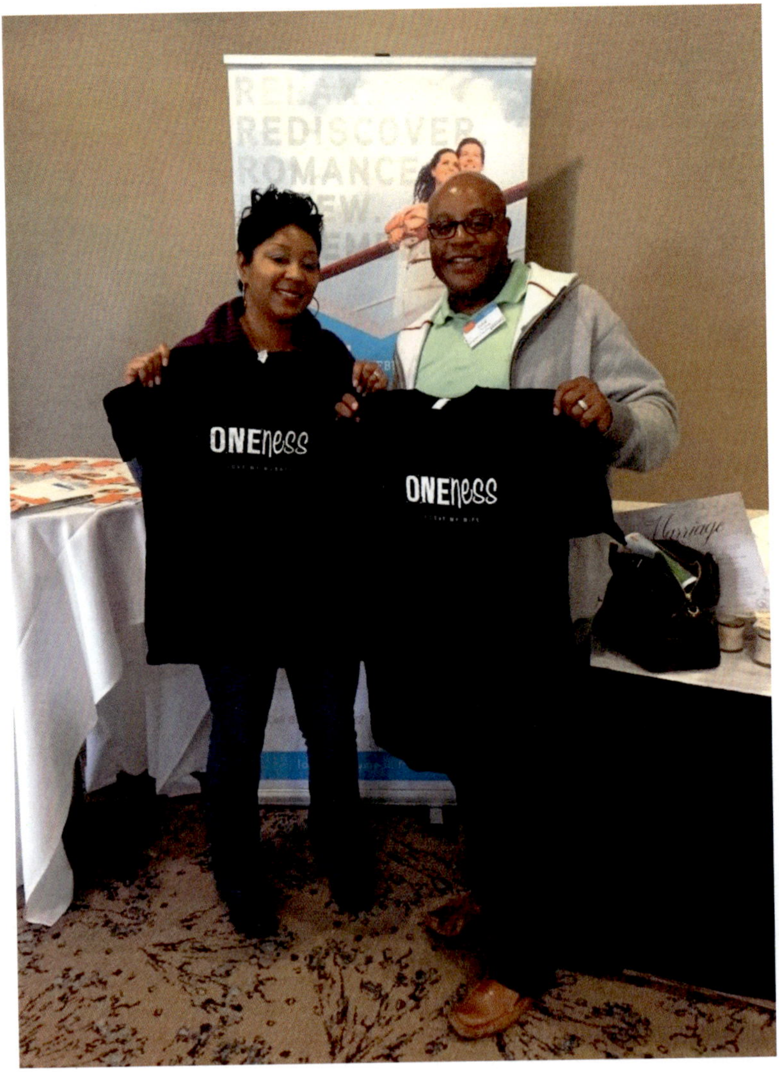
REDISCOVER
ROMANCE
ONEness
ONEness
Marriage

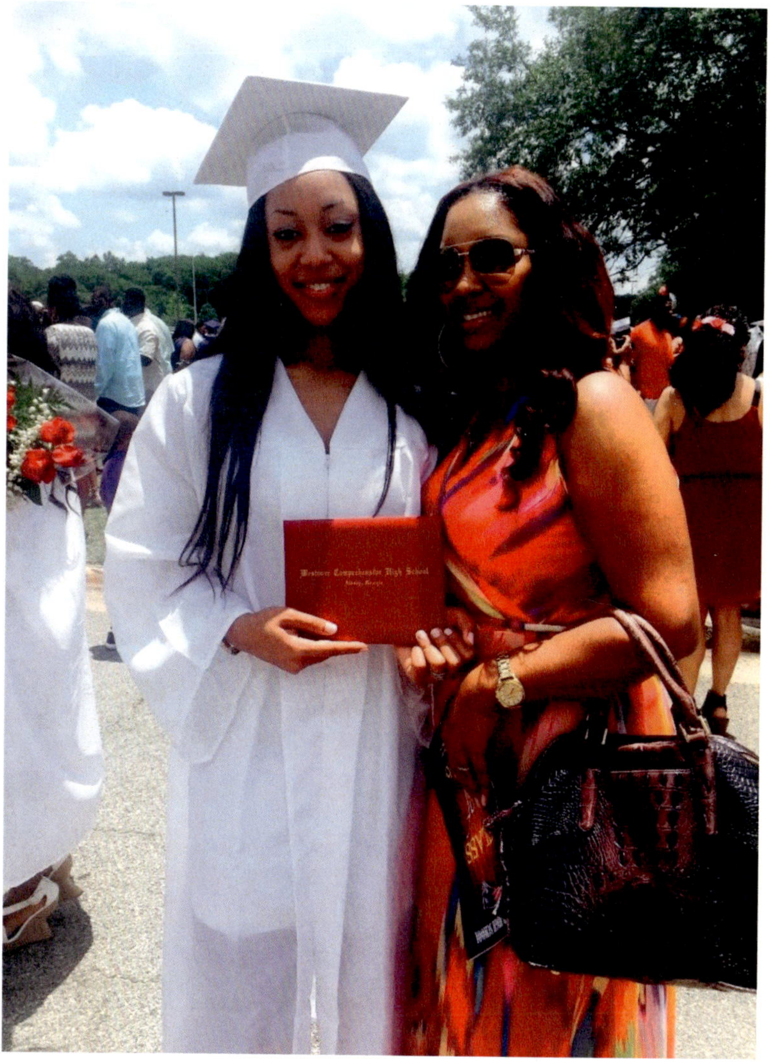
High School

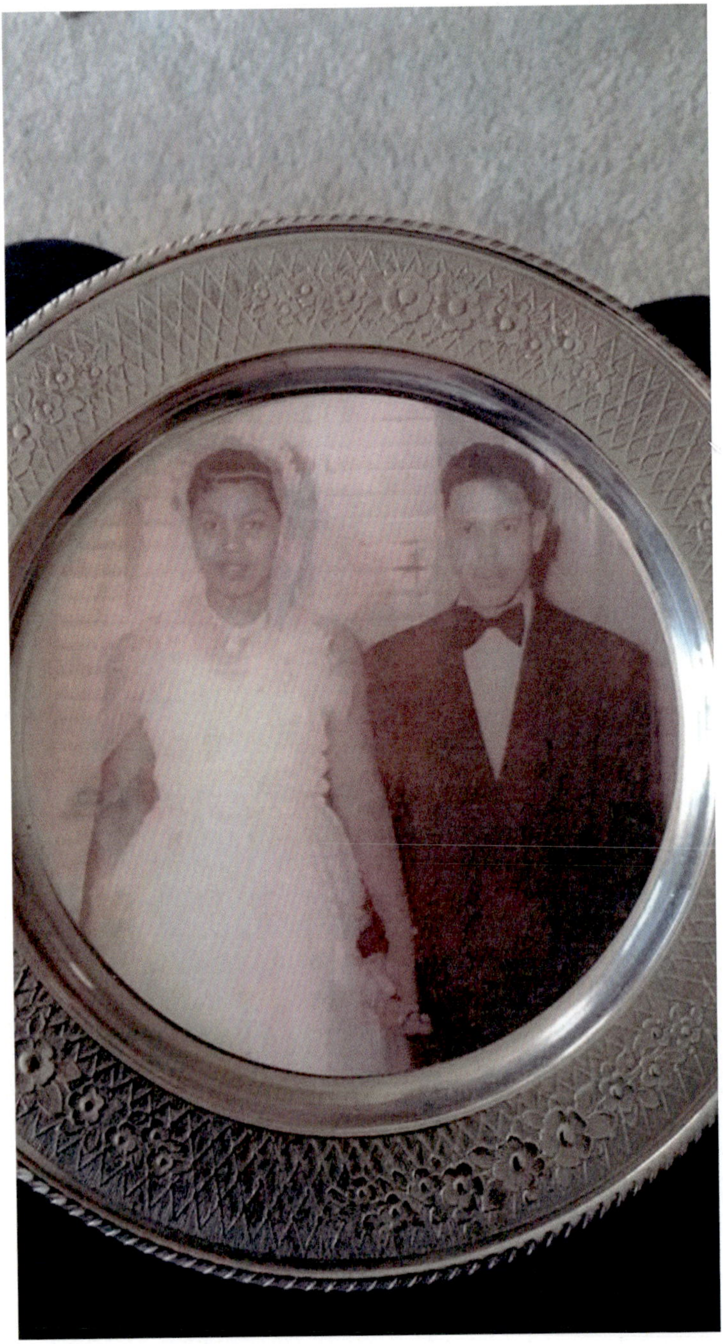

RickyGammagePhotography
www.RickyGammage.com
770.380.1421

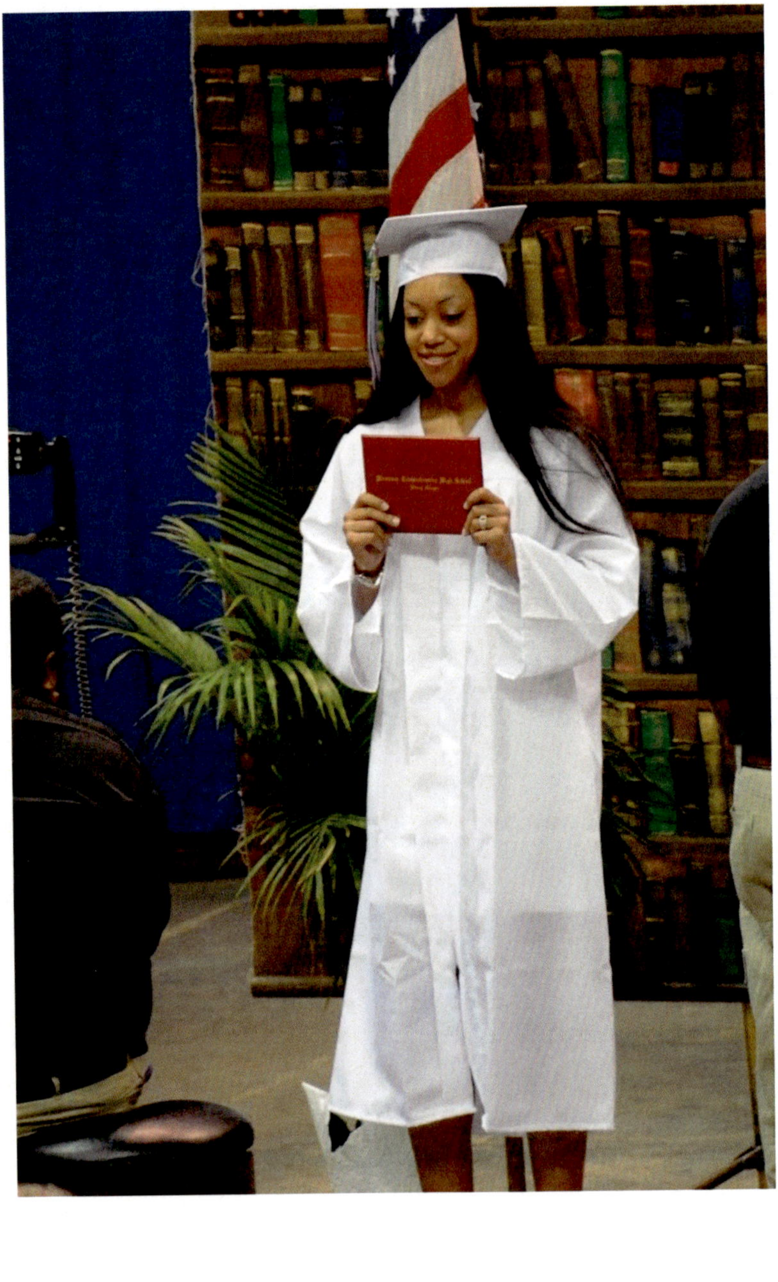

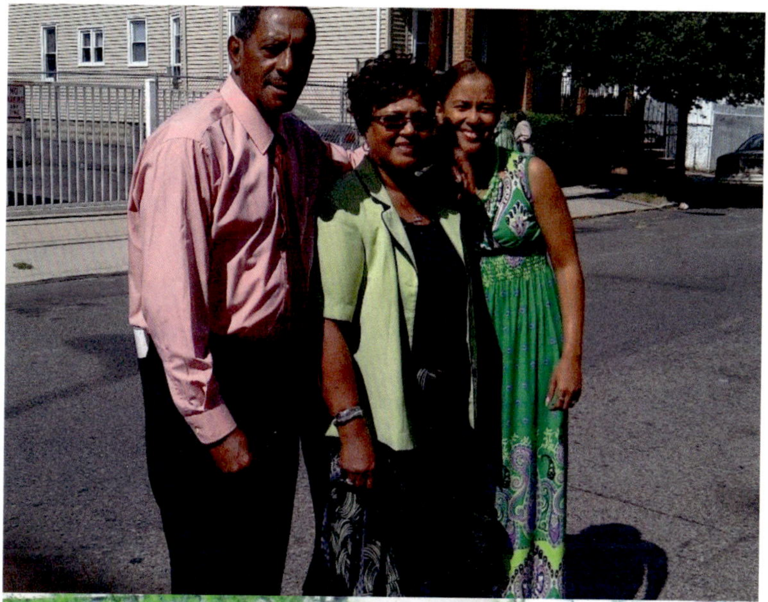

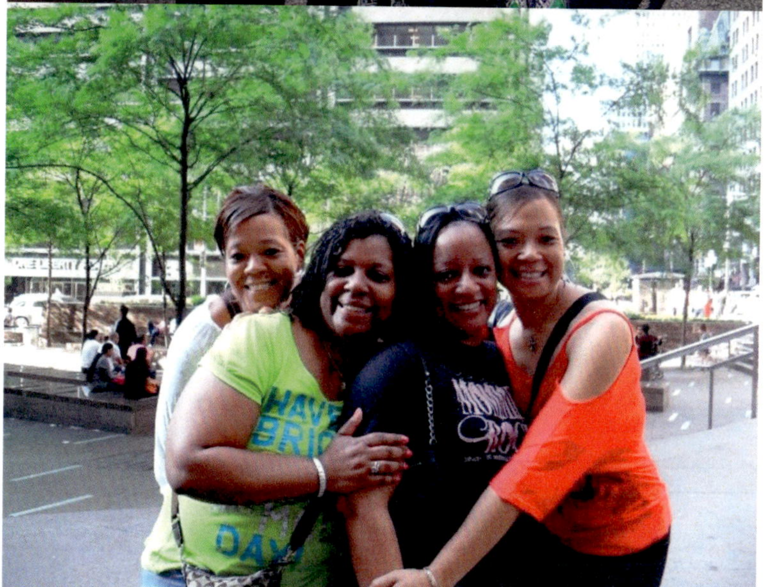

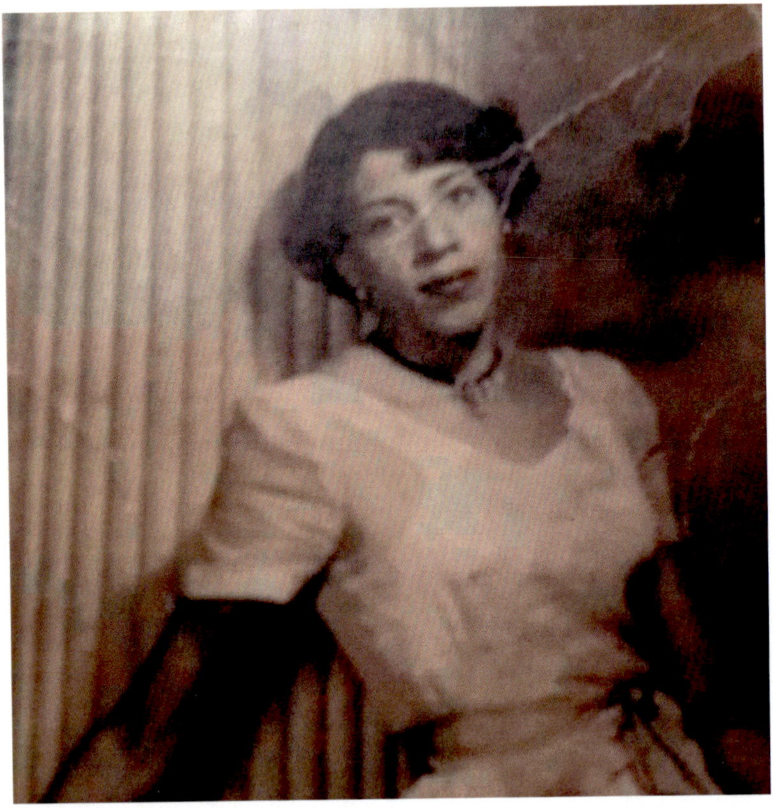

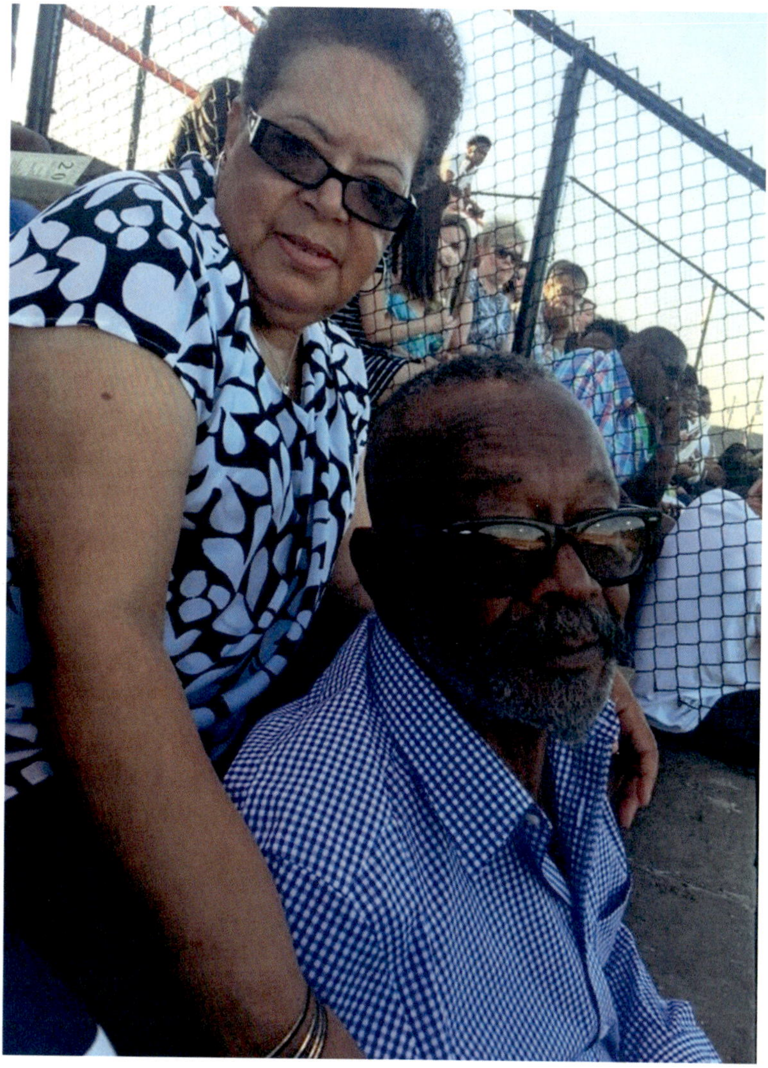

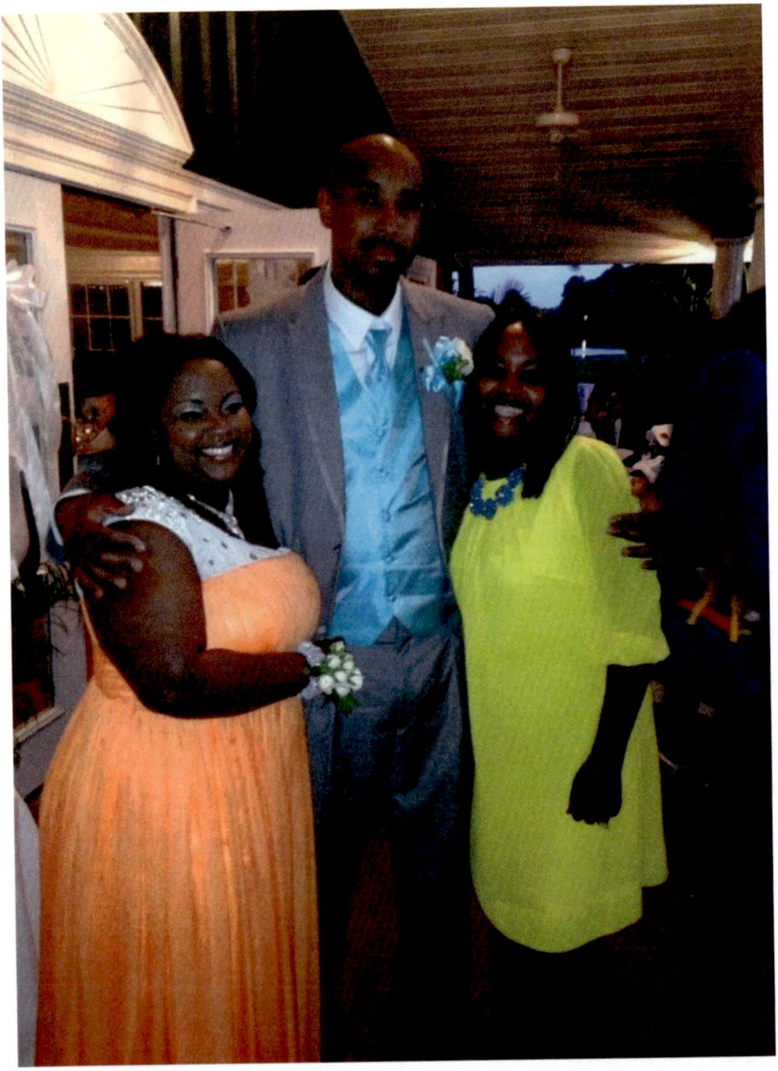

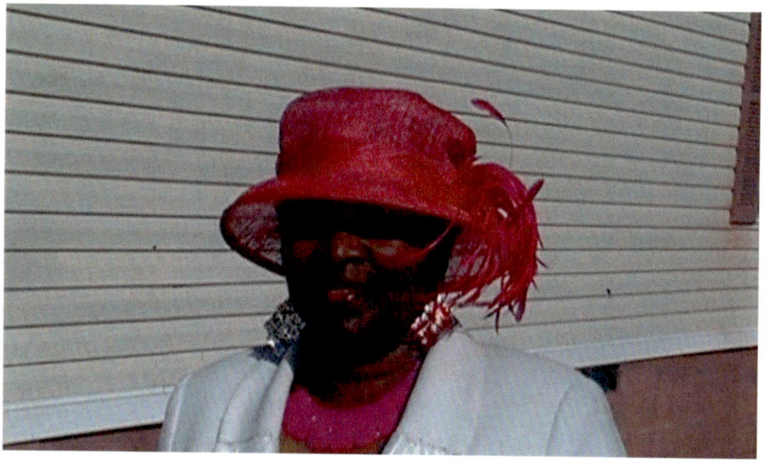

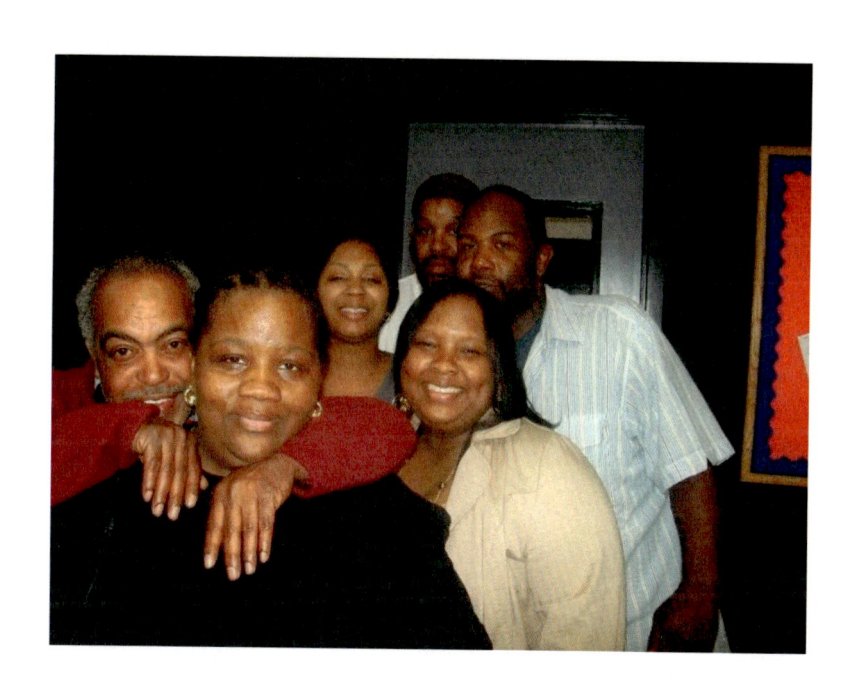

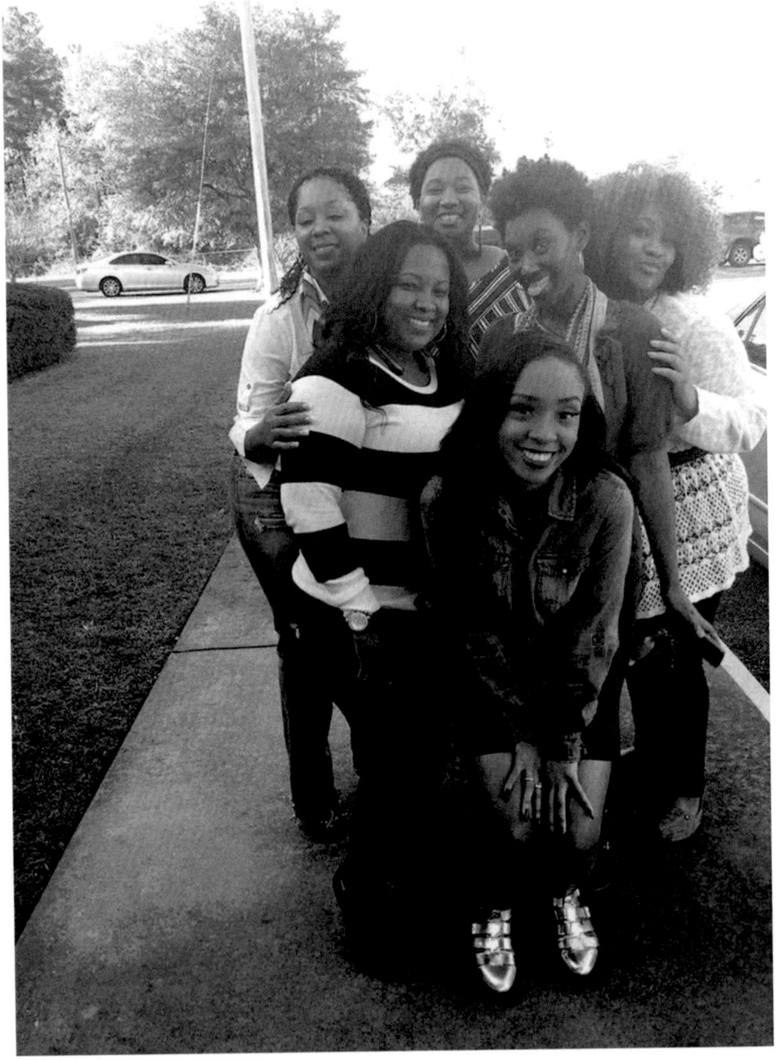

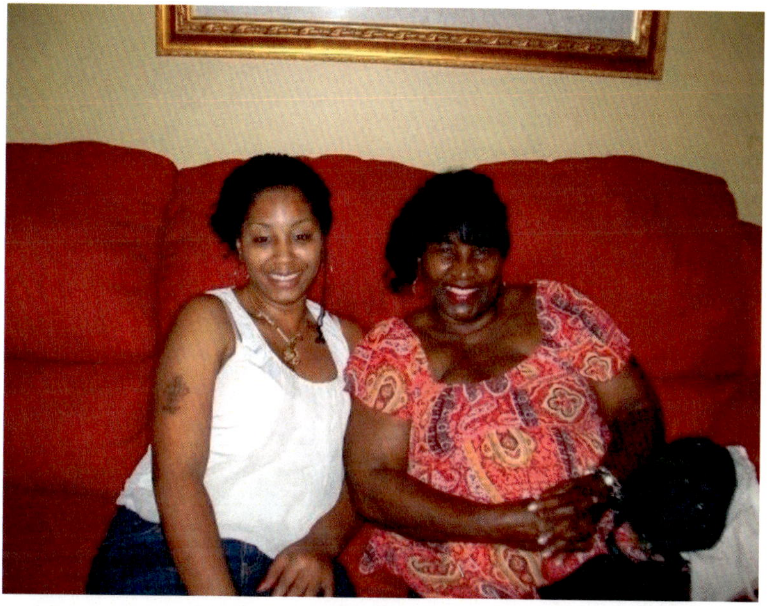

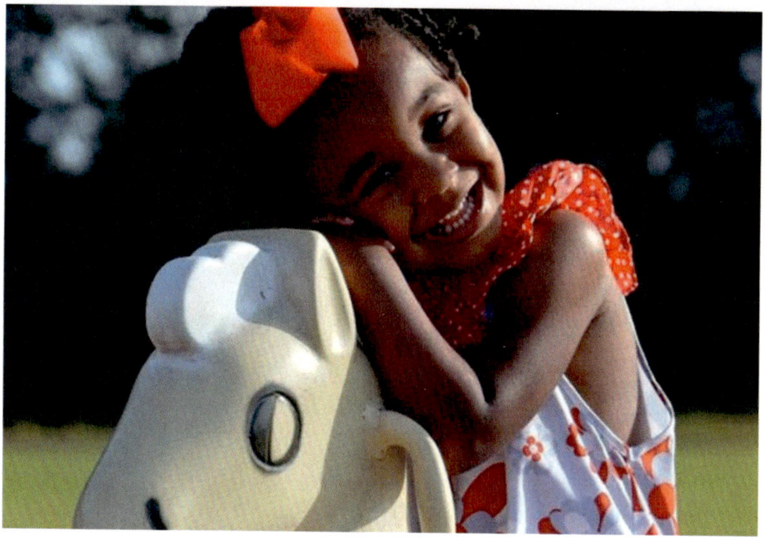

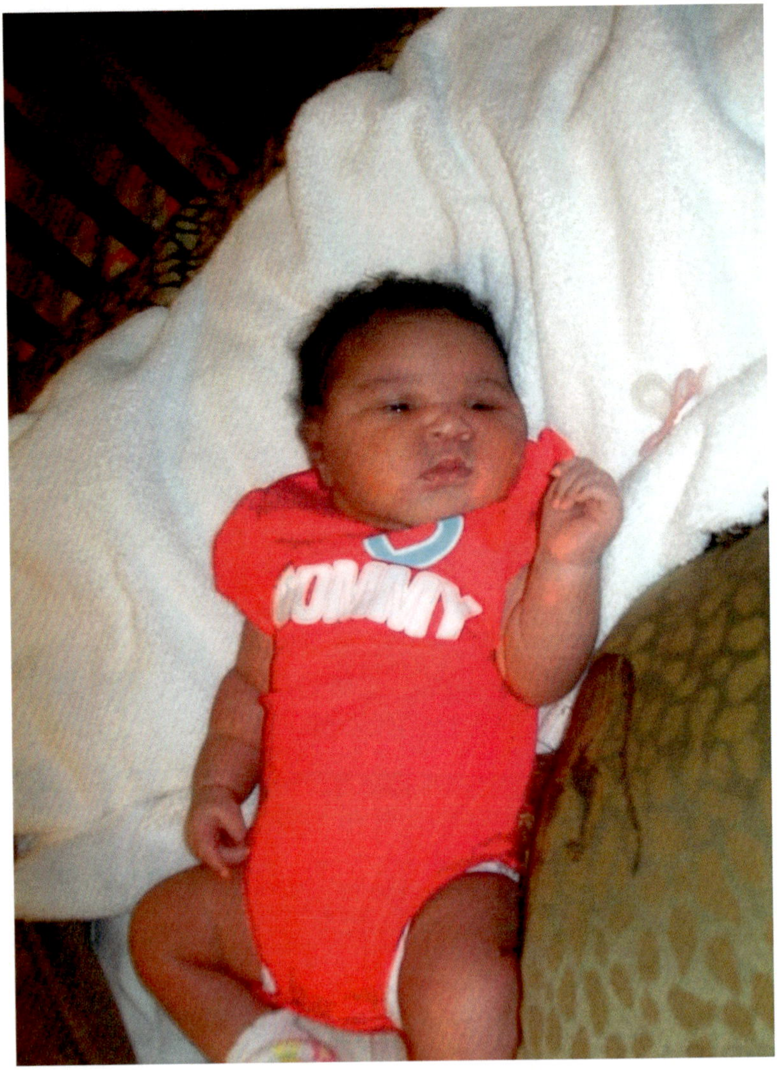

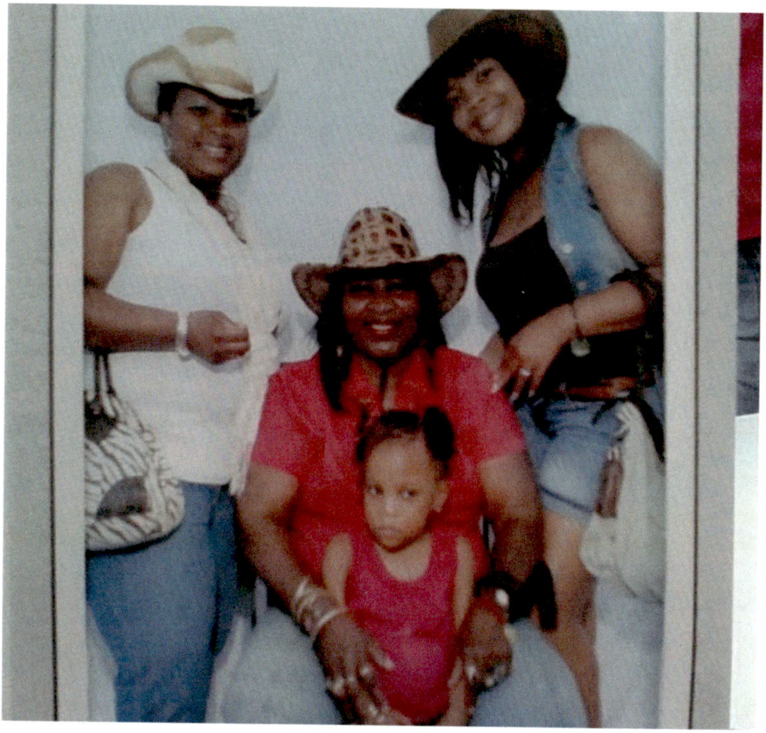

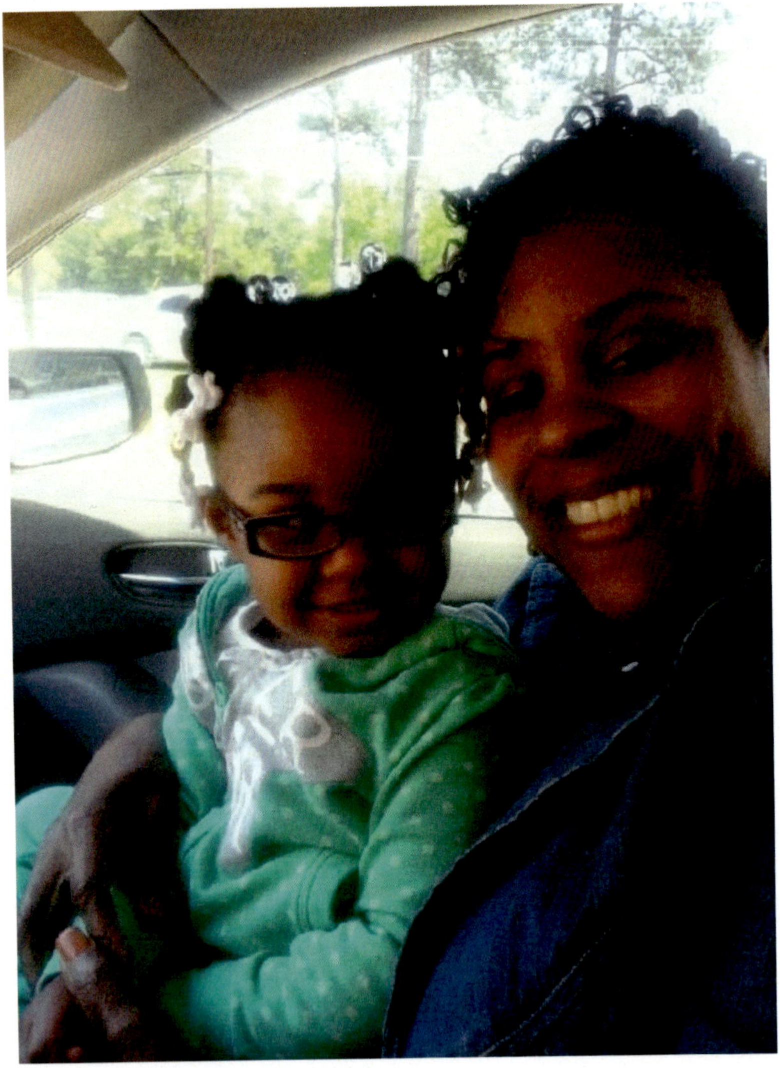

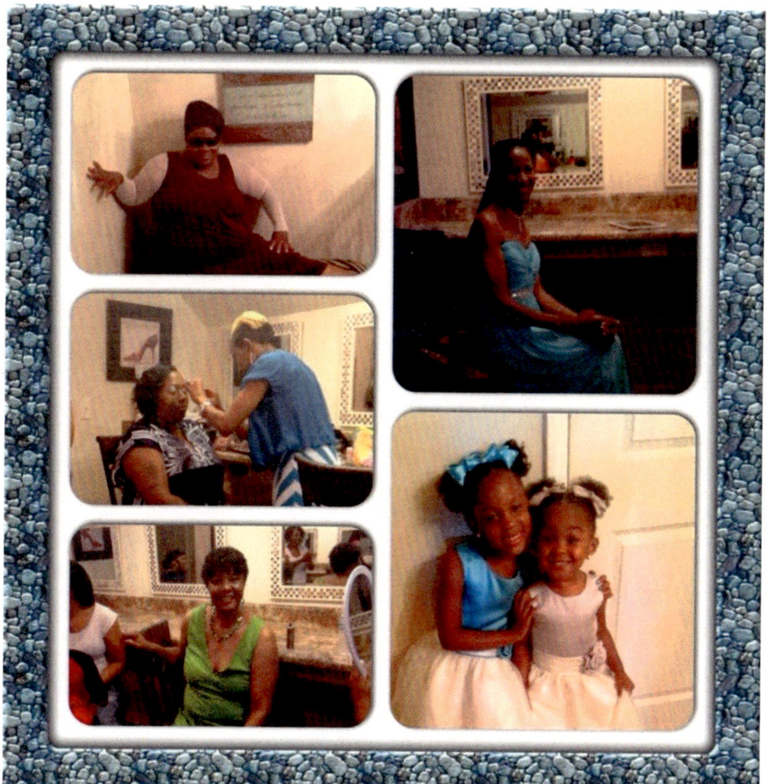

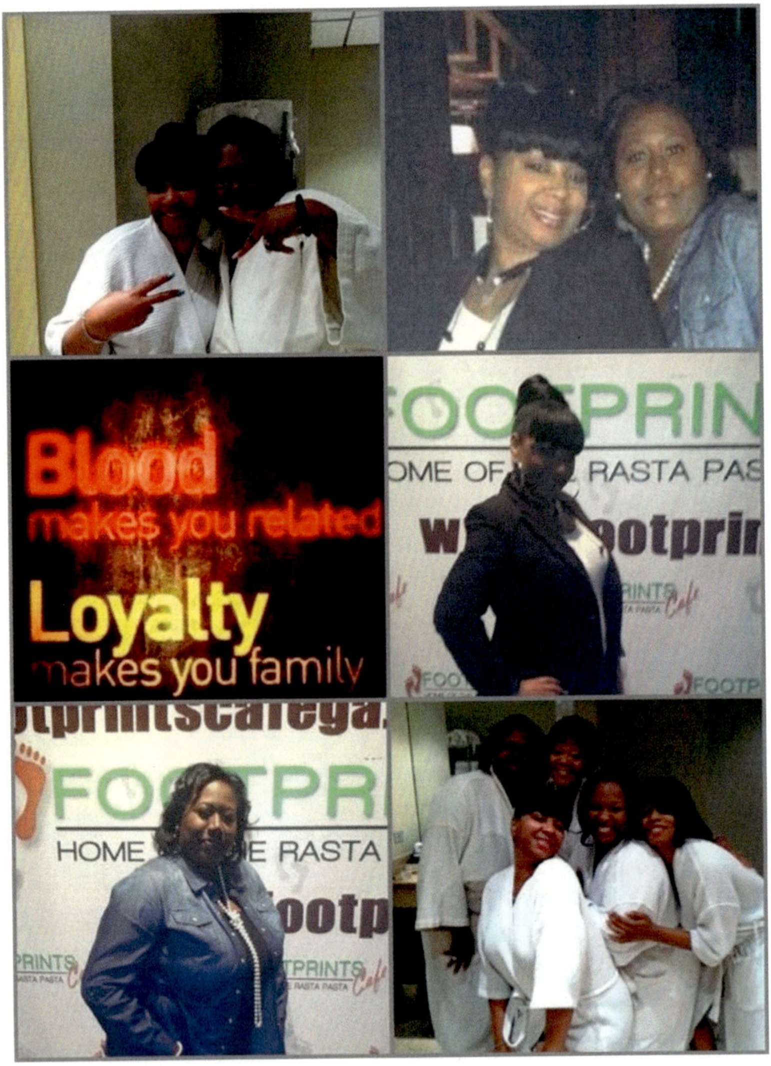
Blood
makes you related
Loyalty
makes you family

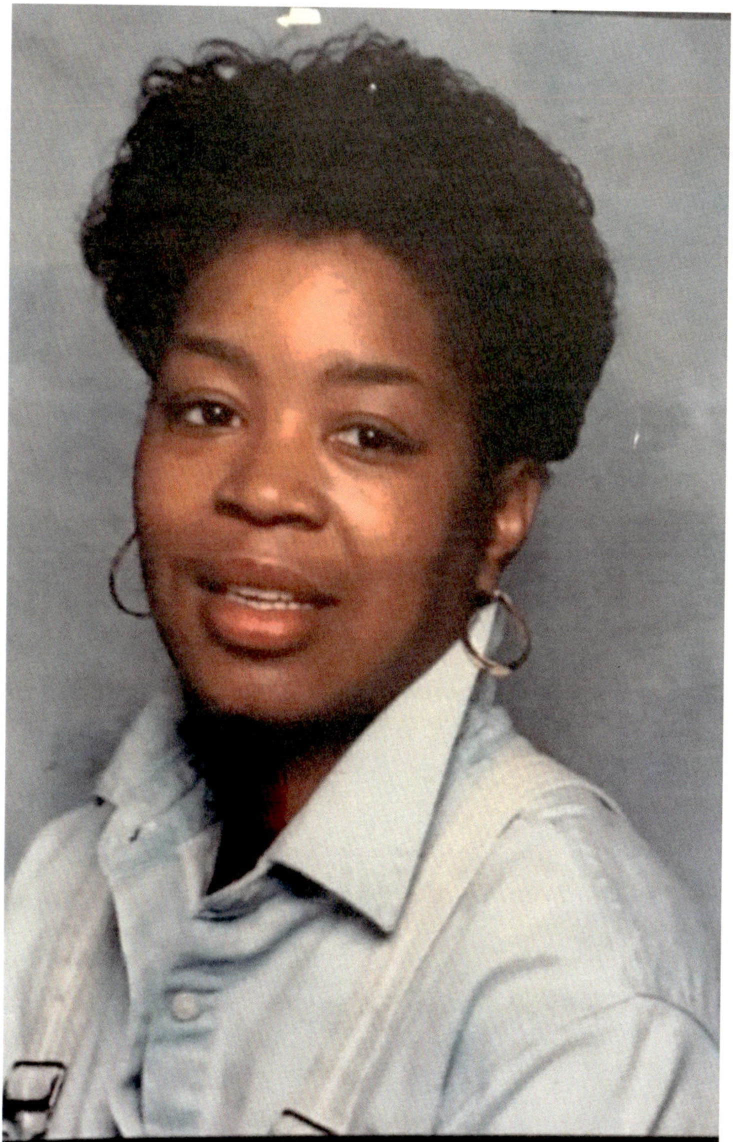

Gideon replies, "If now I have found favor in your eyes, give me a sign that it is really you talking to me."
-Judges 6&17

Chapter 6

Gideon Experience

After relocating to Albany and with absolutely no money in my savings, I knew that I would face many challenges. I did not know to what extent, but I knew I would encounter some. My girls were so young at the time, four and six I believe. I had to find a job that offered benefits, and I needed to find this job like yesterday. I remember putting in applications everywhere, all over Albany. I was attending Albany Tech at the time, thinking that I was going to pursue nursing, but I had to quit the program because I needed to find full-time work. I remember before I started the nursing program at Albany Tech, I had to take a test to enter in. I prayed and prayed for favor on the test because the first time I did not pass it. I was only going to be able to take it once more. Well, I took the test and far exceeded the score I needed to enter the LPN program at Albany Technical College. I was so excited. However, the excitement did not last long. The bills were still coming and I had two little mouths to feed. I decided to put in an application at Phoebe Putney for the hundredth time, and this time, I prayed and asked God to grant me favor. I was always a go-getter, one who just did not take no for an answer easily, especially if it was something I believed in. I called the Human Resources office, and I practically begged the HR lady for a job. My mom used to tell me, Ayesha, you have to sell yourself because everybody is looking for a job. So that is what I did. I told the human resources lady that I was a single parent in desperate need of a job. I told her that I would work any shift and that I needed a chance to prove myself. Well, needless to say, I started at Phoebe March 2003. My first job was a certified nursing aassistant (CNA). This matched well with me, since it is in me to help people and I was going to school for nursing anyway. The first night at work, I lost two patients and had to prepare both of them to go to the morgue. So I guess one can conclude that I was broken in on my very first night of work. I worked in that department as a nursing assistant and a unit secretary for a little over a year. I then moved on to work in the emergency room as a registration representative. Then on to the Carlton Breast Center, next on to outpatient diagnostics, then to internal medicine, then to the billing department, and my last area, which happens to be the seventh department that I worked in, was the business office. Every department that I worked in at the hospital were divine assignments from God. I was in some of those departments to sew a seed and then there were some departments that someone sowed a seed into my life. When my season at Phoebe was coming to an end, I started having all types of dreams and signs. It took me a while to finally surrender and step out on faith. I knew that God was getting ready to transition me, but I was acting like Gideon, the prophet. I just kept needing sign after sign. I was not ready to surrender and walk away from my job, by faith. 1 Corinthians 2:10 tells us that "there are some things God has revealed to us by his spirit. The Spirit searches all things, even the deep things of God." It had been revealed to me, by the Holy Spirit, who knows all things, that my time had come to an end. When God speaks, we need to listen and obey. We do not need to try and figure it out, question him and become fearful. We need to trust that our Heavenly Father knows what is best for us at ALL times. My season had ended because he had plans for me that are greater than any plan that I could ever come up with on my own. Proverbs 19:21 says, "Many are the plans in a person's heart, but it is the Lord's purpose that prevails". I thank God for him doing the directing because I sometimes get in my way. I decided that I had better get going and focus on my relationship with the Father more, to get his work done. I left Phoebe September 2015 to pursue my Master's Degree in Social Work.

Eye has not seen, nor ear heard, nor have entered into the hearts of man the things which God has prepared for those who love him.
-1 Corinthians 2:9

Chapter 7

Overcomer/Restorer

In 2005, I told God that I no longer wanted to be a church hopper and I wanted to be in a church where the word was being taught and broken down to me so that I could, not only understand what was being said to me, but I also wanted to grow. I had seen so much in churches, and I was to the point where I almost wanted to give up. I did not believe that there were any true sold out, hungry, authentic pastors, that taught truth and would not compromise. I wanted my children to grow in the word and I wanted my cousin who was living with me at the time, Ken, to turn his life back to God. I felt that I was very responsible for every soul in my house. I had a night vision, and in this night vision in which I was at this church with a lady pastor. I remember in the dream I saw people going up to the front laying money on the alter. I had only about twenty-eight dollars in my purse at the time. So I told God I was going to lay my money at the altar as well. I did not know at the time what this was I was seeing, because I had never seen this before. Well that next Sunday, I woke my family up and I told them that we were going to Trumpet of God. This was the only church that came to my mind that had a lady pastor. In times past, I had visited the church but I was not ready to surrender, so I do not think I stayed the entire service. However, this time, I knew in my spirit that this was where my family and I was supposed to go that morning. From the moment I stepped foot into the church, I had this feeling of relief. The atmosphere was set; it was like nothing I had ever seen before. The praise team was singing and the banners were being raised. However, this was not it. All of a sudden, as the pastor was speaking, I saw people walking up to the altar laying money on the altar. I looked in my purse to see what I could go put on the altar. Although I was not sure what I was doing, I knew that I had recently had a vision of the exact experience. I had the exact amount of twenty-eight dollars that I saw in the night vision a day prior. I knew without a doubt this was confirmation that we were in the right place at the right time and that my footsteps had been ordered by the divine. Over the next few years, I began to be taught the word in a unique way. It was as if God said, daughter, I am going to give you exactly what your heart has been desiring. "Blessed are those who hunger and thirst for righteousness, shall be filled." (Matthew 5:6). I learned so much in the years that I was at this church. I grew in the word like never before. My eyes were opened to the things of the Lord, as I had never been taught the word like I was being taught. I saw God start to do things in my life in every area. My hunger and passion grew more and more. I began to read and study the word of God more and more. I remained at Trumpet until I got remarried in 2014. My life would never be the same, not because of a church, please hear me, but because of the obedience of the pastor and the grace and mercy in my life. For this, I will forever be grateful.

The steps of a good man are ordered by the Lord, and he delights in his way.

-Psalm 37:23

Chapter 8

Grace and Mercy

There are times that we know that God is working things out in our lives and we see his hand on our lives, yet we still will not surrender our everything to him. It is like the children of Israel: they would complain, and God would deliver them. They would complain again and again, and God would grant them a favor by delivering them time and time again. I knew that God had used me in many ways, and he was still using me, but that did not stop my flesh from wanting to rise. So, therefore, instead of me "Seeking first the Kingdom of God and all of its righteousness", I began to seek things, such as men. I wanted to date, after all, I was single right? I started to slowly fall back into that state of temptation by making wrong choices. In any relationship, the other person is either drawing you or you are drawing them. There is no in between, and this is where we get into trouble. The dates were not healthy for me at all. However, Satan's biggest deception is to make something look and feel so good so that we are pulled in so deep that we could not get out if we wanted to. It would take a divine intervention from Jesus Christ to get untangled from the hands of the enemy. I knew that I was what one would call a lukewarm Christian. I stopped studying the word like I once had. I stopped wanting to be around all of the saints like I once did. I was truly going through the motions and all at the same time putting on facades, because as long as you look the part you do not have to be the part, right? Well, this is so far from the truth, although many will fail, because they just want to look good, and could care less about being right. I was sending my soul to hell quickly and non-stop. I would feel awful for the sexual impurities that I was involved in. I would repent, then turn right back around and do the same thing. What I did not realize at the time is that true repentance, means to do a 180 degree turn, to turn away from those sins and not return. What I was doing was feeling bad for the moment. I had not yet truly repented, and that is the reason it was so easy for me to go right back to what I was doing, even if that meant a few months later. I will admit that there were times when I thought, "okay I got this. I can handle myself without falling into temptation." I thought I could outsmart the enemy and, *yes*, I was wrong! Not wrong because he could not be defeated, but I was wrong because I was not fighting with the right weapons. I was not casting down all those imaginations that eventually trapped me. The word tells us to "cast down imaginations, and every high thing that exalts itself against the knowledge of God" (II Corinthians 10:5). I had to learn the hard way. It was all a part of my journey. What I learned is that not many are willing to discuss these kinds of real issues in the church. The only time sex will come up in the church most times is when one is either trying to condemn or convict a person by telling them what will happen if you fornicate or commit adultery. At some point, we have to have real discussions by allowing people to open up about where they truly are in their walk, without them having to worry about being condemned. God is a God of conviction, not condemnation. The way one will know if they are being convicted or condemned is that, condemnation draws us away from God, but conviction draws us toward the father. I had to get real with myself and confront my shortcomings if I was ever going to be set free for real.

For in this hope we were saved. Now hope that is seen is not hope. For who hopes for what he sees? But if we hope for what we do not see, we wait for it with patience.

-Romans 8:24-25

Chapter 9

He That is Without Sin

I met my youngest daughter father at a time when I was no longer looking. As a matter of fact, the way that we met was divine within itself. I was working at one the hospitals offsite clinics after hours when the last person who left the office forgot to lock the front entrance. I sat in my desk working and trying to hurry up to get home to my children, especially since it was way past the five o clock hour. I heard the door close and a voice say "hello is anyone here". I stood up from my desk which happen to be on the opposite side of the wall, so he was not able to see me right away. I then peeped through a small window to ask this young man if I could help him. He then preceded to tell me that he was new in town and rushed over to the office to try and find him a local doctor. I walked around to where he was standing and told him that we were actually closed at the moment but if he called the office the following morning that I would be glad to help him get an appointment. I gave him the office number and my name and then he took off. I did not think anything else of this at the time. The following morning at approximately 8:15 am the office phone rang and the gentleman on the other line politely asked if he could speak with Ayesha about making an appointment. I then made the gentleman a same day appointment. Once he came in for his appointment and had seen the doctor, the last stop would be yours truly to check out and or schedule another appointment. He thanked me for getting him in so quickly and we made small talk. He told me he was from Brooklyn and I told him I was from Jersey ironically. He then left the office to return the following day for lab work. At this appointment we once again made small talk as he was checking out and I asked him what was he going to do in the good life city of Albany that weekend, he boldly said, hang with you. I laughed he laughed and I thought to myself, no way I am not looking for that type of relationship. I am content and no need to start nothing unless it's serious. Well low and behold I decided to take him up on his offer but not without giving him the run down. I told him that I do not go out anymore, but I would be glad to show him around Albany and show him where the clubs were. He said okay and so he picked me up that Friday night and we rode around showing him Albany. We then went to dinner and had just great conversation. I felt like I had been knowing him all my life. Yet I was still not attracted to him nor was I thinking about a relationship. I thought that he had good conversation and he thought the same for me. Over the next several weeks we began to learn more and more about one another and I found out that he was once on fire for God, but due to hurt and past stuff, he had pretty much stop pursuing Christ like he once had. I had so much compassion for him, especially since I know what it's like to have church hurt yet know that you need to be in fellowship with other believers. I would pray for him that God would draw him back to him and that he would give him his hunger and zeal back that he once had. Well after spending time together almost every weekend, we decided to take a break and allow him to get his life on track and I no longer wanted be a hinderance, especially since we started having feeling toward one another. Neither one of us were in a position for this at the time. Well we stayed away as long as we could then started back seeing one another, and since I would not allow my flesh to remain on the chopping block, I found myself in a situation, which I thought at the time, was the worst situation ever. When I found out that I was pregnant, I felt awful. I felt that I had failed not only my children, but I felt I failed everyone that I had ever witnessed to, either by my life, or by word of encouragement. I felt that God was not ever going to forgive me for this horrible thing I had done. I did not want to go to church. I slowly stopped going and became depressed. I could not believe that I was in this situation. Especially since I was not having a lot of sex right? Well, that did not matter; the fact that I was having sex and I knew I could get pregnant. I finally told my daughters, and this was one of the hardest things that I ever had to do. I did not want them to know that I had failed in an area that I thought I had overcome. In the beginning, they were shocked and a little disappointed. It was not long before they began to accept it for what it was. I remember being in my bedroom alone having a pity party, and the Holy Spirit started speaking to me. He reminded me of the woman that was caught in the act of adultery; everyone wanted to condemn her for the sin she had committed. However, Jesus made one request of her accusers, "he that is without sin cast the first stone". Everyone began to drop their stones because they had all sinned and fallen short of the glory of God. Therefore, they all walked away and left the woman standing there with Jesus. Jesus told the woman, "Neither of your accusers can stone you so neither can I." But it was the last words that he spoke to her that ignited something in me so strong when he spoke the very same thing to me, it was to "Go and Sin No More". When I heard this, I fell on my face and cried out to the Lord. I knew then that he had given me another chance. He had forgiven me for my sins. He was allowing me to be made whole again. I was so broken and so hurt and felt all alone. However, he reminded of his covenant with him. I began to hear the word Journey over and over again. At the time, I did not know I was going to have a girl. All I thought was the Lord is taking me on a journey, and this is the path he is allowing me to go. The following week, I had to go to my doctor's appointment to see what I was having. The doctor told me that I was having a girl and immediately I was reminded of that word I heard in my bedroom, Journey. I began to thank God for the blessing that he had allowed, and I started to turn my life completely back around. I discovered the true meaning of the word repent. My daughter's father and I did not have sex anymore for the next three years. I had made up in my mind that just like the woman caught in the act of adultery, I was going to go and sin no more. I told my daughters father this and he had no other choice but to agree, as he saw how serious I was and how important this was to me.

The righteous person may have many troubles, but the Lord delivers him from them all.

-Psalm 34:19

Chapter 10

God of a Second Chance

My youngest daughter's father, Derek, and I went through our valley experience for three years. During this time, God had begun doing a new thing in Derek. I told him that sex was not going to be an option any longer and that I was giving my life completely back to God. I was not going to allow anything to cause me to waiver. I had many conversations with him asking him to get back into a relationship with God. I did not want anything to happen to him while he had not yet truly repented. I would pray and ask God to turn his Derek's heart back to him. What I did know about Derek, was that he really wanted to get his life back on track with the Creator. He was just in a place that he needed to be healed and set free from his past mistakes, failures and hurts. You see at the time I was thinking I could help him do this, but then I would become his god. So, I had to step back and be obedient to the father but not having sexual relations with him and be the woman of God that I knew God had called me to be. Then and only then could the father work on this man and do a new thing in him. However, at the time I did not know how or when God was going to do it, but all I knew is that I had a word from the Lord, and I was not going to play with it. Derek would constantly be invited to church by one of his coworkers, but he would never go. One day, just out of the blue, he called me and told me that he was going to church. I could not believe it; I knew that God had heard my cry, but more importantly I knew that God's Grace and Mercy was with Derek. It was not long that Derek's life started changing for the better. He started throwing away all of his old R&B cds and buying Christian music. We started having godly conversations and for the first time, I began to feel that we were getting on one accord. Derek started sharing with me all the wonderful things he was learning at Victory Tabernacle, and then he started helping with the Sunday school classes. I started to see his life change before my eyes. I knew that the God of a Second Chance, was allowing the both of us to get this thing right. No, it was not because we were perfect people, but we were obedient people that turned and did a complete 360. One day Derek set up a date for him and I to go on a dinner cruise. I told him yes, because I had always wanted to go on a day dinner cruise. However, there is something about a woman of God who can see things in the spirit. I had a dream a few weeks before Derek asked me on this dinner cruise, that he had given me these beautiful earrings. So when he asked me to go on the cruise, I thought about that dream, but immediately brushed it off because I thought, "no way he is going to try and propose to me with a pair earrings." Well, we went on our date that evening on Lake Blackshear. It was a beautiful evening, and the sun was shining just right. We both were excited about the cruise. There was another couple that sat with us who was very friendly. After eating our dinner and listening to some nice music on the boat, Derek walked over to the guy that was sitting at our table and asked him to record something with his phone. I was looking at him like, "what are you doing?" Derek came back near me and bent on one knee; I was shaking like crazy because I could not believe this was happening. Derek began to quote some scriptures out of the book of Solomon and then asked me to marry him. I said yes, of course, and he presented me with this beautiful ring. Everyone on the boat was clapping and saying congratulations to us. I felt so special on this night and every night since. For the next year, Derek and I would continue to work on ourselves individually so that there would be no mistake about what we believed God was joining together.

Shortly after this, I asked my pastor if she would christen, my baby daughter, Journie. She agreed and asked me to be prepared to share some of my testimony with the church. This was, of course, after I had repented and gone back to the church to make things right. I started researching Journie's name for some reason to be prepared for my testimony that Sunday. I came across the Hebrew-Greek meaning of my daughter Journie's name. The root meaning of her name in Hebrew is Derek. I could not believe it, how could this be, that I had a child out of wedlock, named her Journie and I discover a year after she is born, that her name and her father's name are tied together? This was Biblically amazing to me! Some things that seem foolish to the world are not foolish at all to God. He knows the end of a thing from the beginning. He knew the mistakes and the failures we would make, yet he turned it all around for our good. I remember that day of our daughter's christening, that I had to share my testimony. I was very transparent and of course a little nervous. However that day after service there were people who told me that our testimony really blessed them and that it had helped them. They thanked me for being transparent. I knew once again, that it's not about what you go through it's about how you go through it and come out of what you go through that matter. We all are going to go through things in our lives but we must know that our stories will help others, therefore we cannot be afraid to share our story.

"You are never too old to set another goal or to dream a new dream."

-C.S Lewis

Our Big Day

Derek and I married on June 14, 2014. Our wedding was held in a small town outside of Moultrie, GA. We were married at Gin Creek Plantation, where everyone was able to stay in cabins and enjoy one another for the entire weekend. Our wedding colors were pool blue, silver, orange and ivory. It was very beautiful and the staff were very accommodating. The atmosphere was perfect. Derek and I had gone to the property on several occasions praying on the property. I believe that we have the ability to set the atmosphere no matter where we are. I must brag on my Boaz for a moment, my husband, Derek, is a great man with lots of love for his wife, or what he calls his "good thing." (smile) I can honestly say that Stephanie Mills said it best, "I never knew Love Like This Before". I thank God for the man of God that he has blessed me with. Derek is very patient toward me and truly loves me for me. Our wedding day was special because the Father allowed a lot of my family members as well as Derek's family and church family to attend this occasion. There were family members at the wedding that I had not seen in over ten years. It was such a blessing and honor to have that many family members celebrate with us on such a joyous occasion, alive and well on a joyous occasion, rather than on a sadder one. Too often, when that many family members get together, it is due to a death, unfortunately. Although my biological father was not alive to walk me down the aisle, his brother, my uncle Gerald Beckwith, represented to the fullest. On this day, I married my best friend, What a MIGHTY GOD we SERVE!!

The Father truly makes all things new when we submit and surrender our hearts to him. He is truly a God of a second chance. He is Lord of ALL; the beginning and the end; Alpha and Omega, Prince of Peace, healer, restorer, deliverer, sustainer, vindicator, judge, chief physician etc. If you don't know him; if you don't have a relationship with him, today is the day to make a decision. John 3:16 states, *"For God So Loved the World, that he gave his only begotten son, that whosoever believes in him shall not perish but have eternal life."* Why don't you choose today, Christ Jesus? He is waiting patiently. He is not a respecter of person. If he changed me, he can and will change you if you allow him to. Selah

For we all have sinned and fallen short of the Glory of God.

-Romans 3:23

"There is purpose in the pain. The pain was never meant to define you, but the pain was meant to refine you. Stay in the purpose, while enduring the pain."

- (Ayesha T)

Dedication

This book is dedicated to my husband, my best friend, who is always so very supportive of me in everything. He encourages me to be better and not to ever give up. He pushes me to higher heights and deeper depths. My husband who makes me believe that I can do anything and as a team we can do any and everything. I Love You Babe. To my three beautiful daughters, Miesha, Miya and Journie, you all will never know the love that I have for you. From the moment I laid eyes on you, I knew that there would be nothing in this world that I would not do for you. I want you three to be the Women of God that he has created you to be. Never give up on your dreams. Love others unconditionally and pursue Wisdom like nothing else. There is truly nothing like a mother's love. Lastly to my unborn very first biological grandchild, Nova Skye, I love you already, more than you will know. I know that you are going to grow up to be all that the creator has destined for you to be. Remember that you are all more than conquers in Christ Jesus. To my aunt Bert, who sacrificed a lot so that I would have as close to a normal life as possible. Your reward is yet to be given a hundred times fold. Lastly, but definitely not least, My Lord and

Savior Jesus Christ.

If it was not for you destining me from the very beginning of time, calling me out into the deep and bestowing your grace and favor over my life, I would have thrown in the towel a long time ago.

ACKNOWLEDGEMENTS

I, first and foremost, thank the heavenly father for allowing me the opportunity to be able to share some my life story, in hopes that it will identify with some soul that may have given up on hope, love or second chances. I love you Lord, not because of what you have done, but because of who you are. You loved me when I did not love myself. I am grateful to my husband for pushing me to completing my book, and even purchasing my laptop so that I would not have no excuses (smile). I give thanks to my family especially my daughters and friends, because of course without you all, I would not have a story. (love you). To my Pastor Eddie Adams and Assistant Pastor Dennis Eckles. I thank God for you all sowing into my life by sacrificing your lives and sowing into Gods' kingdom. The two of you have helped me in more ways than one. I would be remiss if I did not acknowledge my last pastor, Apostle Charlene Glover. I thank God for your dedication and commitment of training disciples so that we could go out and be the ambassadors that Christ intended. Because of you, my foundation was truly laid and for that I am grateful. Last but not least, I want to thank Mrs. Victoria Brackins for being a vessel used by

God so that I could tell my story to the world. You have been there with me leading and guiding me to write this book with at least pain as possible. Although I did not always meet some of your deadlines, (smile) you did not give up on me. I would have never known that coming to Victory and encountering such a beautiful spirit, that you would be the one to help me with this project. Thank you!

A letter to my younger self,

Dearest Ayesha,

I want you to know that in life there will be good times as well as bad times. There will be times that you will want to give up on life and throw in the towel but know that if you endure to the end, you will finish the race. You are a rare jewel, you are more than a conqueror, you are fearfully and wonderfully made. There is no one that could ever duplicate you because you are unique, this is how the creator intended for it to be. Never listen to the negative words that others speak of you or your parents for that matter. Remember, they do these things because they too are hurt. Hurt people hurt people. Never be ashamed of the parents who birthed you. Remember, you are the person you are because of them. If it had not been for them, there would be no you. God needed the two of them, nobody else, to create the person you are. Ayesha, you have a purpose and a plan and God will surely fulfill his purposes in your life, but only if you step back and allow him to lead you. Friends come and friends go, but do not take it personal, everyone is not meant to go where your going. There will be those that will start out with you but they will not finish with you. Just like you, they have their own assignments. Never try to repay your enemies for wrong, know that if your heart remain pure, God will intervene and make your enemies behave. They will not overtake you but will only cause themselves harm. Ayesha you are anointed and appointed for such a time as this. Surround yourself around positive influences, those that will empower and lift you up and not put you down. Don't allow bad choices to prevent you from going forward. Remember, we all have a past, and it's those past situations that will cause you to grow. The righteous man fell seven times and got back up. Ayesha know that to whom much is given much is required. Stay the course and never give up. Smile more than you frown and laugh more than you cry. Treat others with the same respect that you want to be treated. Embrace your own uniqueness and appreciate every part of your being. You have talents that are yet to be revealed. Never regret helping others who don't always necessarily appreciate your help. When you want to share what's on your heart, share it with the one that matters most first, Jesus. Don't expect for others to approve of you, as long as the creator approves of you, is what really matters. Save your body for your husband, remain a virgin, until marriage for this is sacred. Don't allow guys to use your body for their selfish gain. If you don't respect your body and who you are, no one else will. Know that its okay to be different, after all you are a child of the most high God. You are the called out one, you are a peculiar people, a royal priesthood. You are a reformer and you love righteousness over unrighteousness. Pray everyday, by first thanking God for his many blessings, those that you see and those that are yet to come. Read God's word daily and meditate on it day and night, then you will have good success in life and be prosperous. Selah

Sincerely,

Ayesha

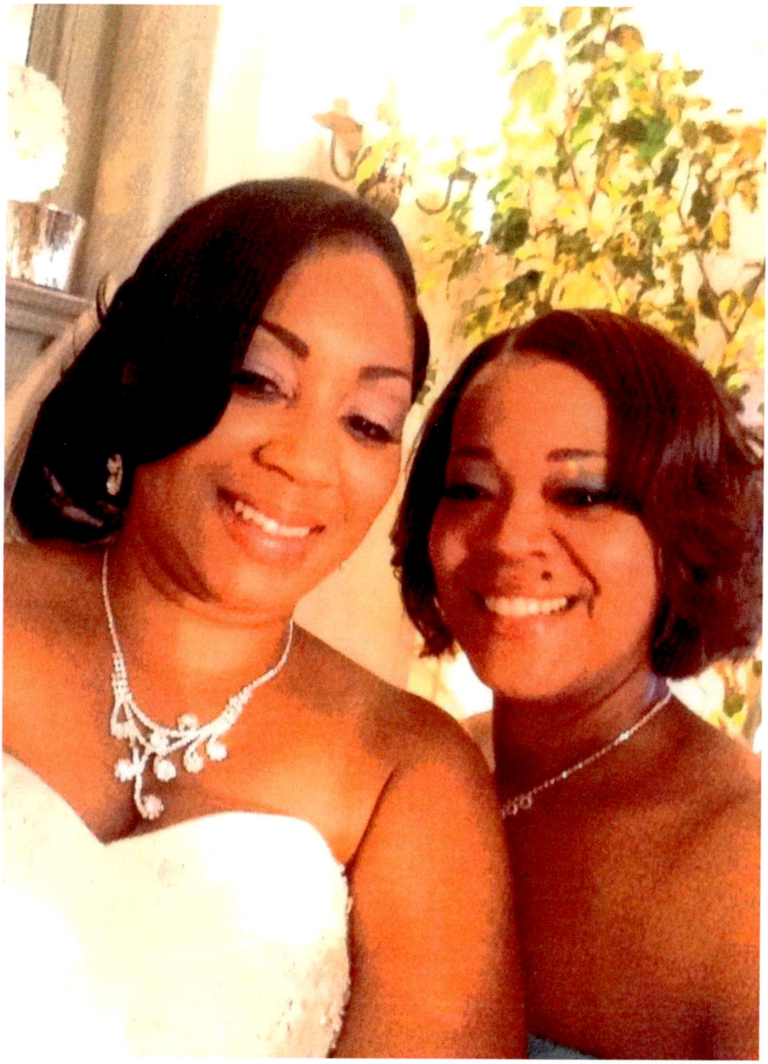

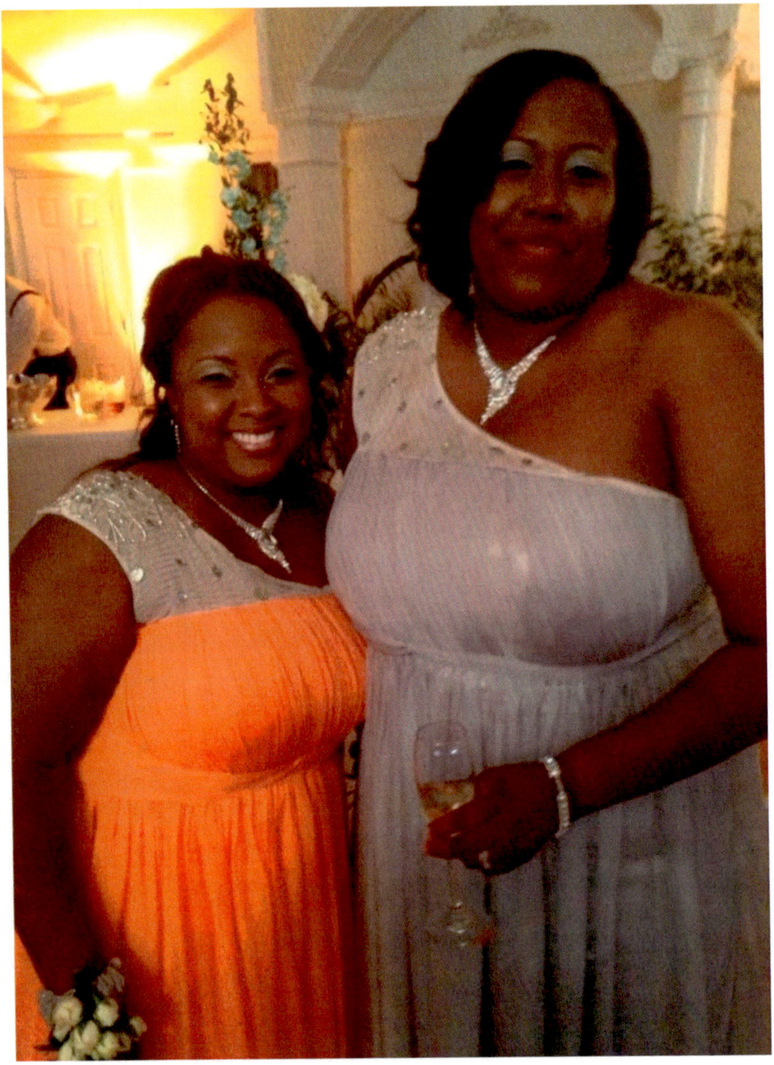

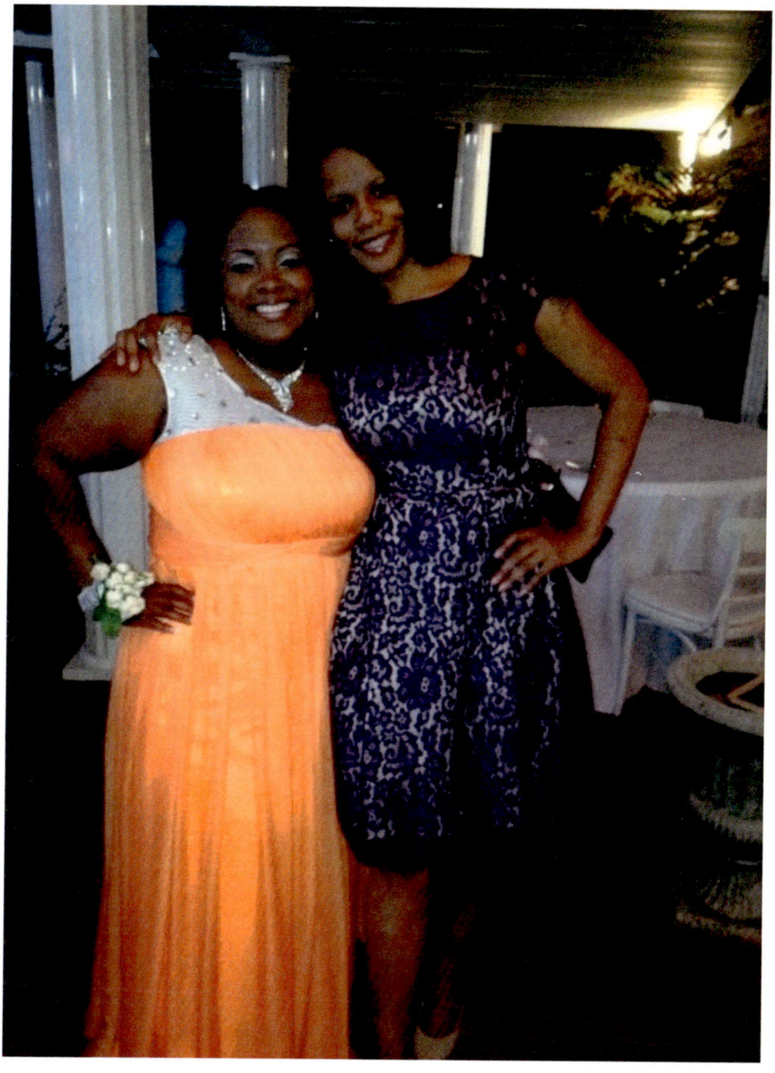

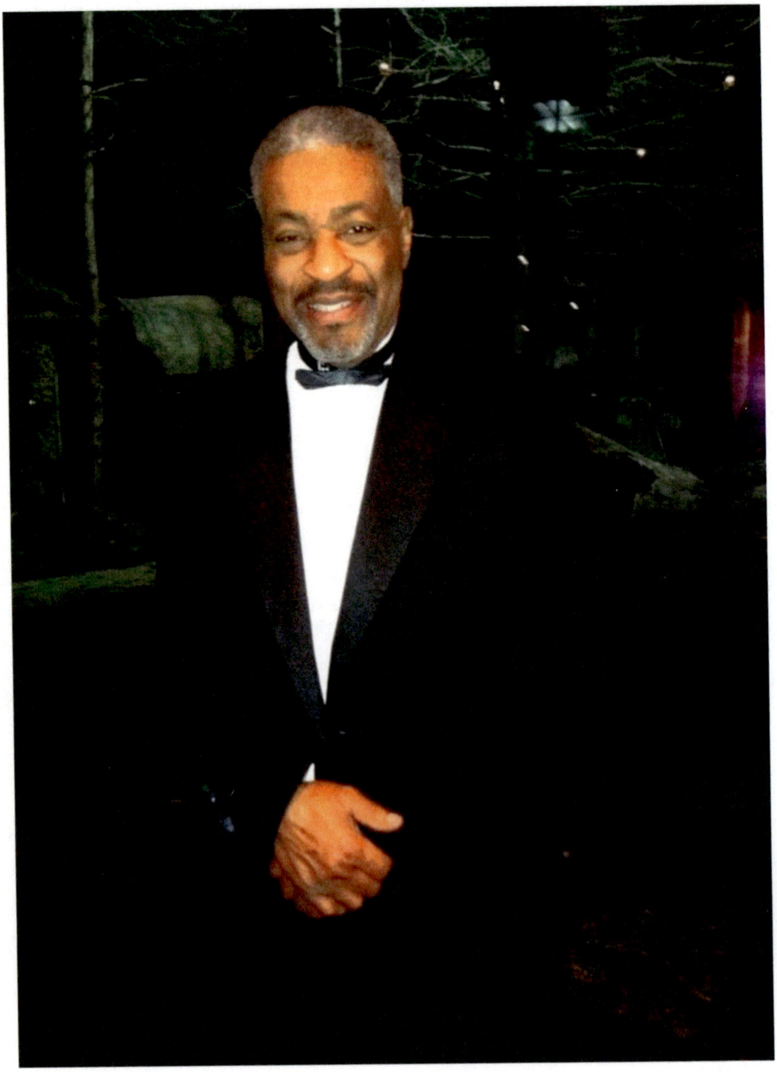

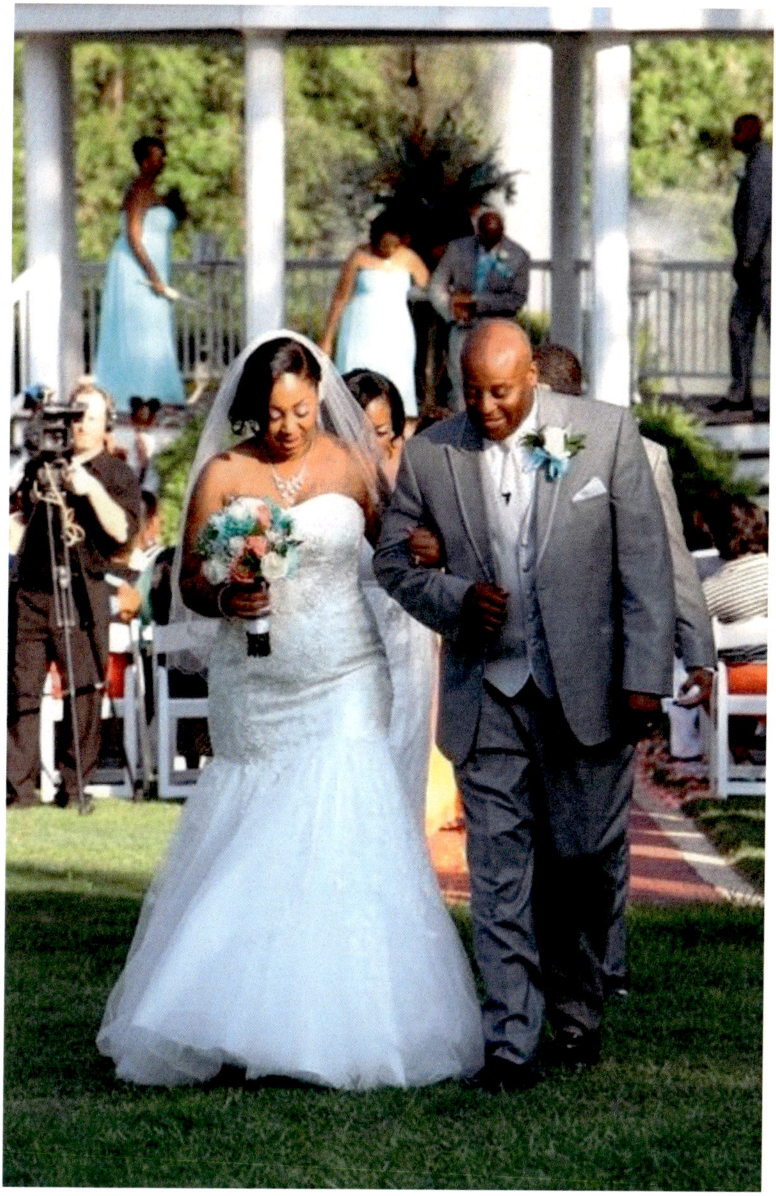

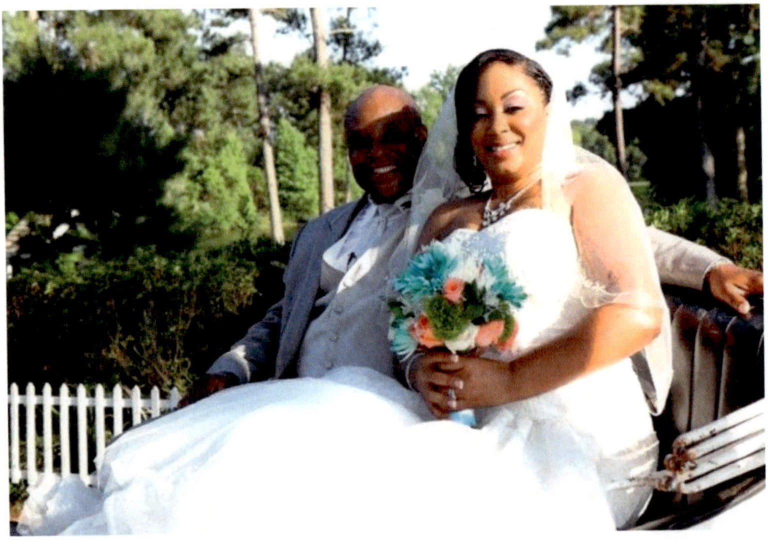

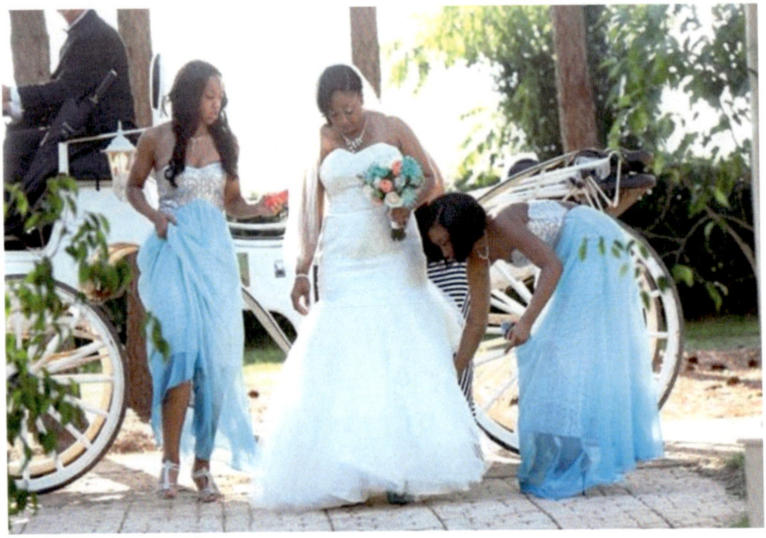

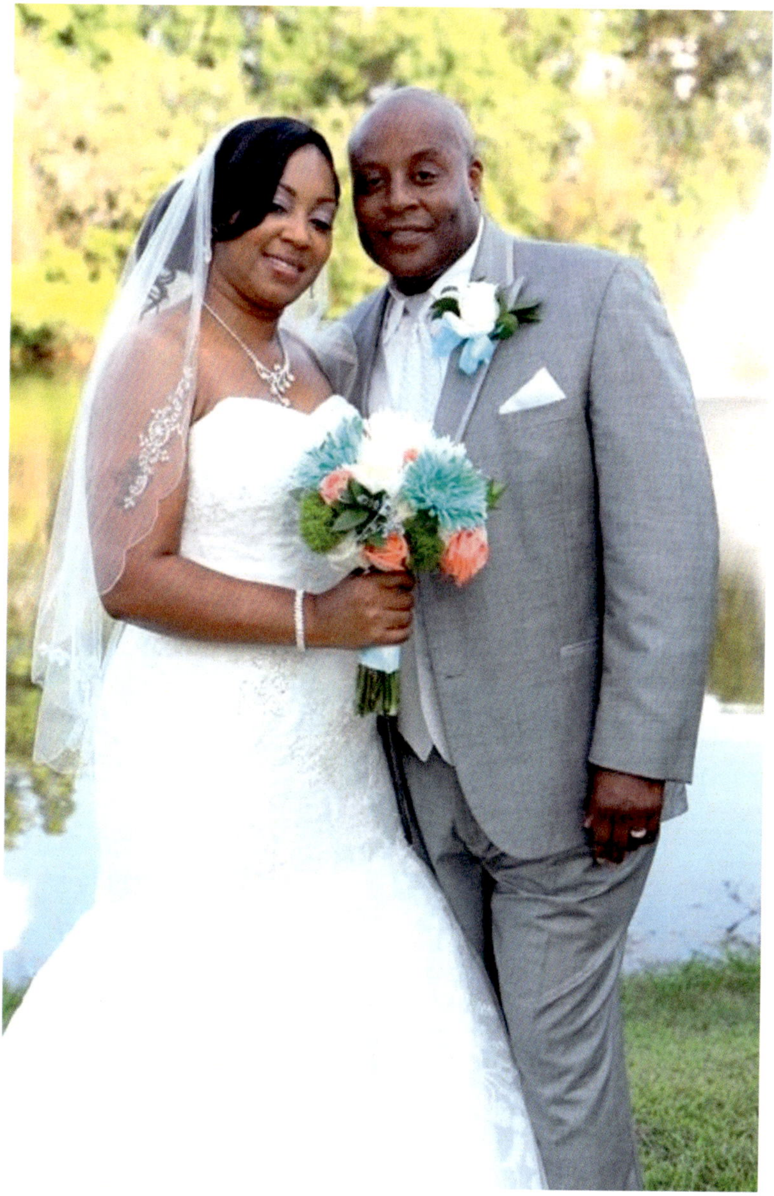

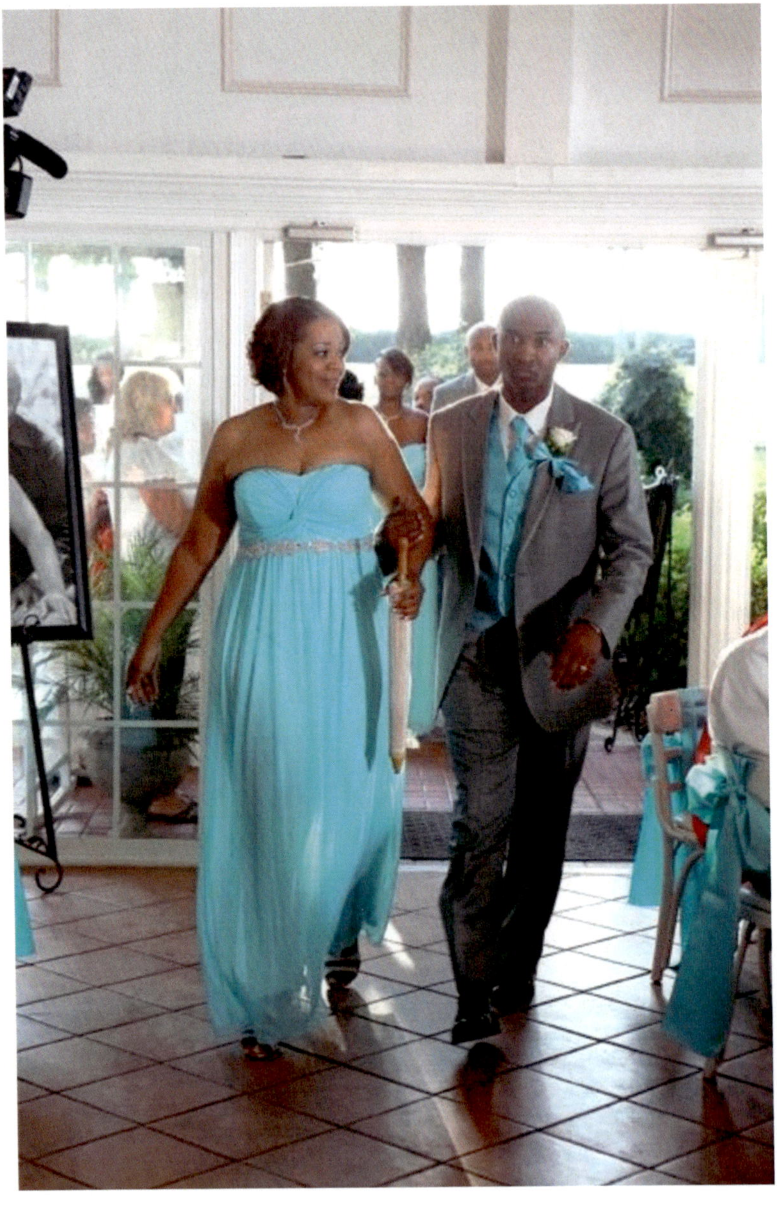

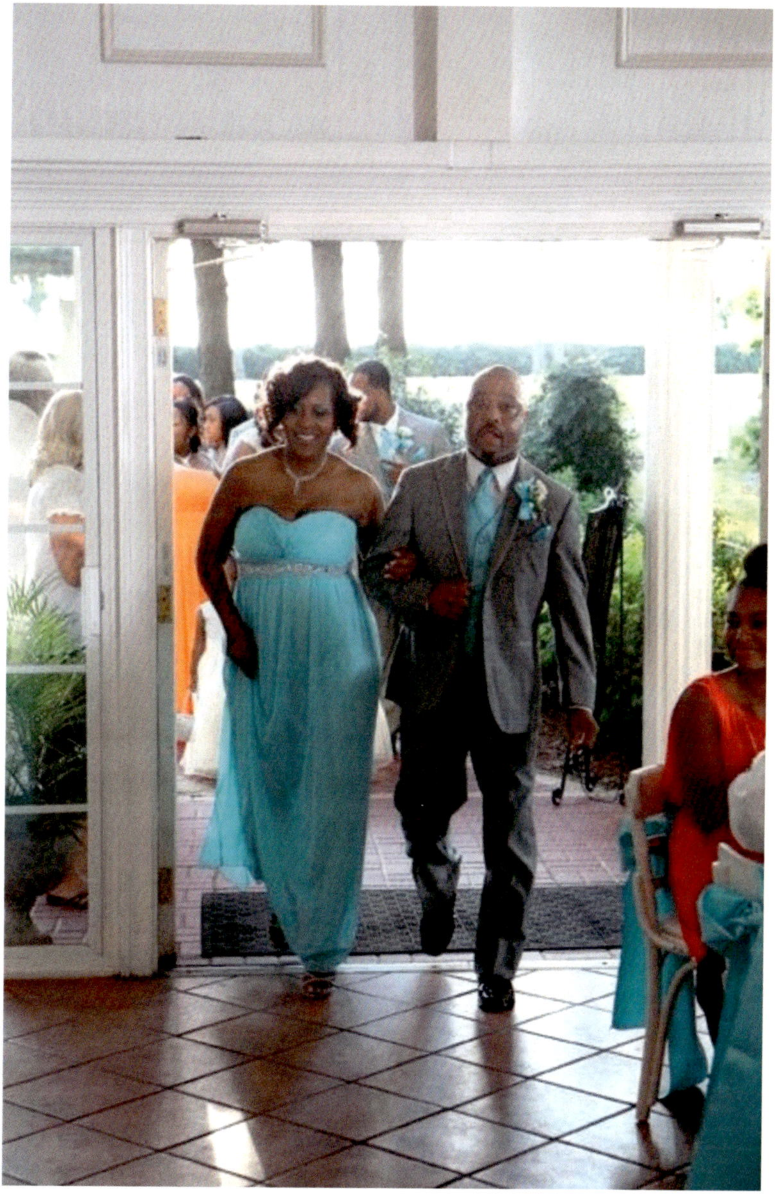

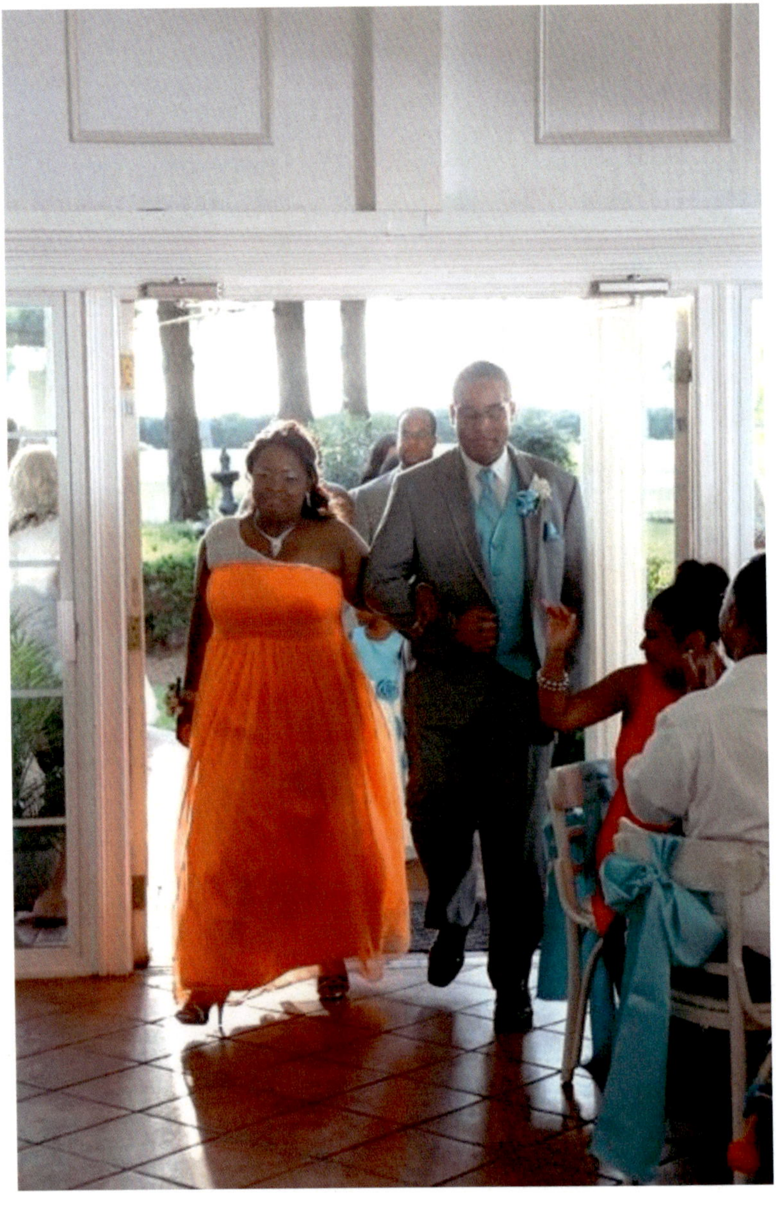

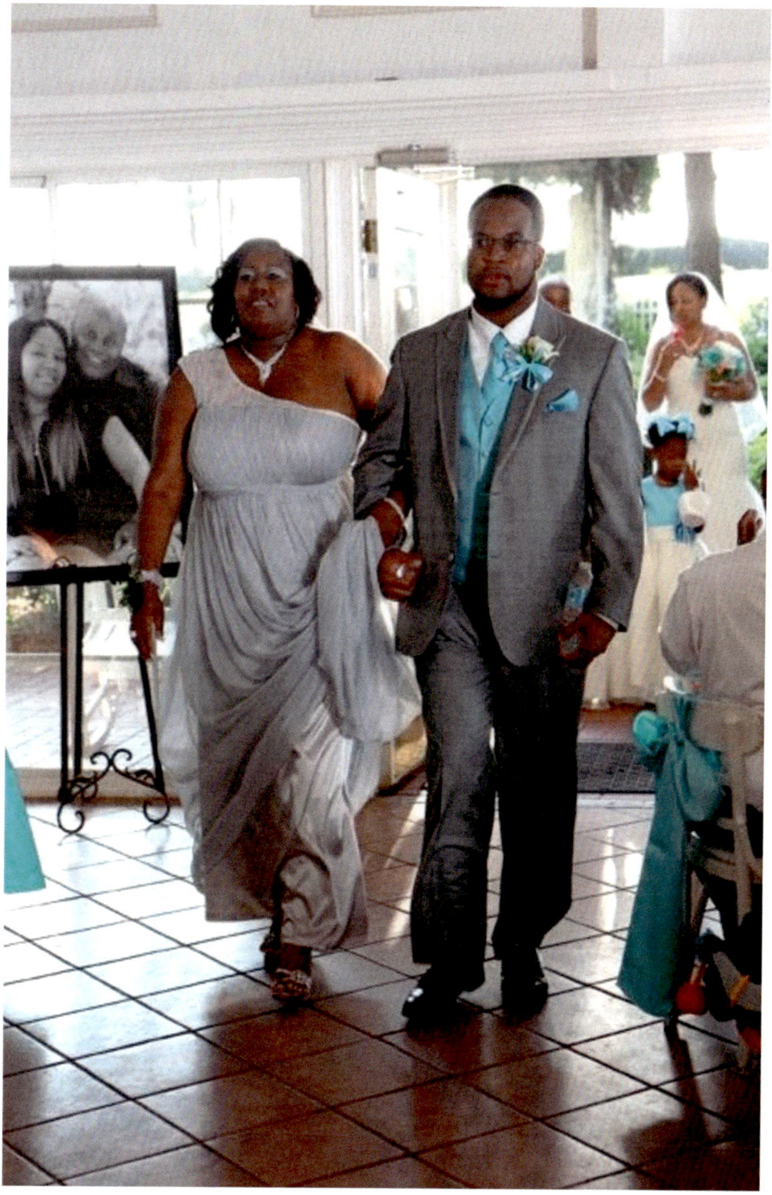

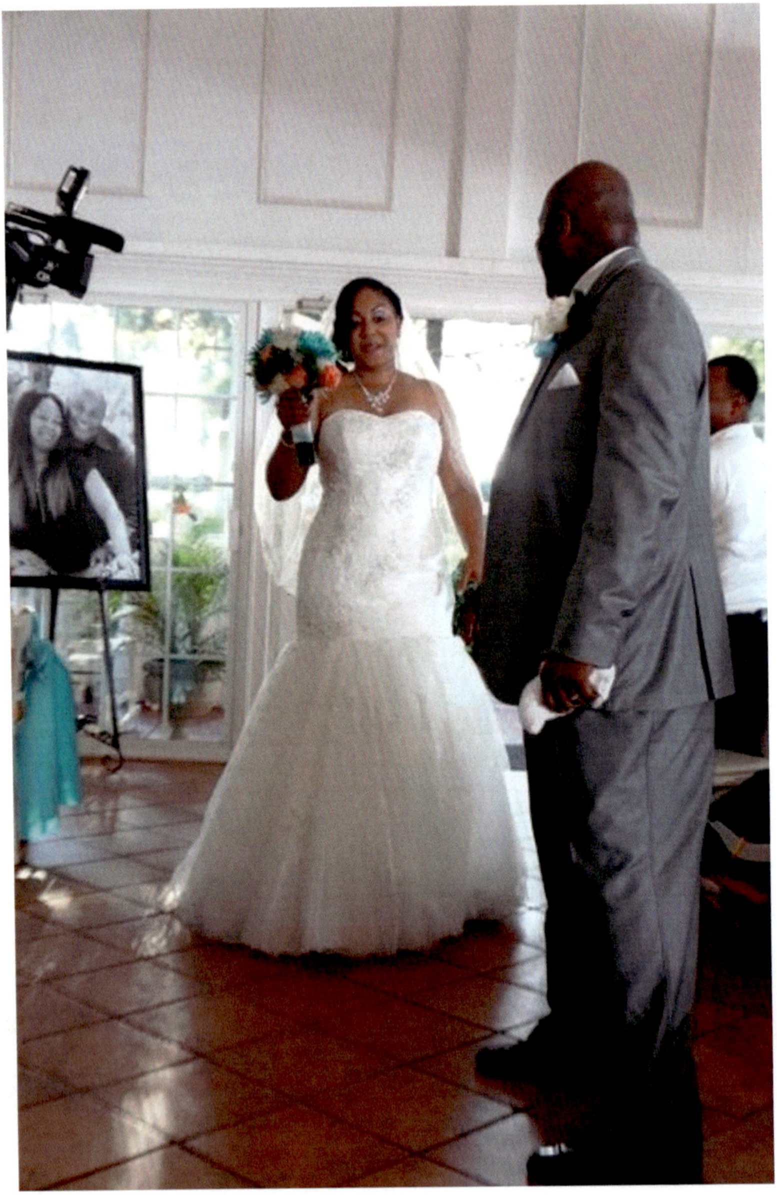

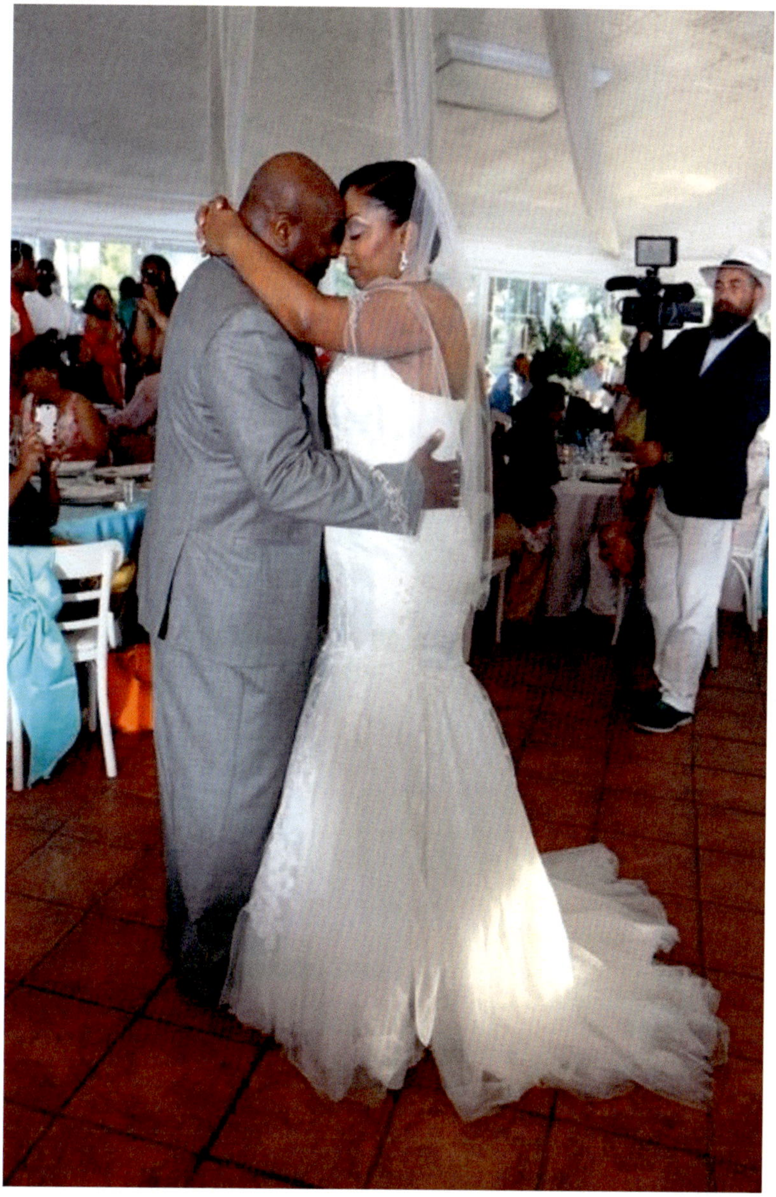

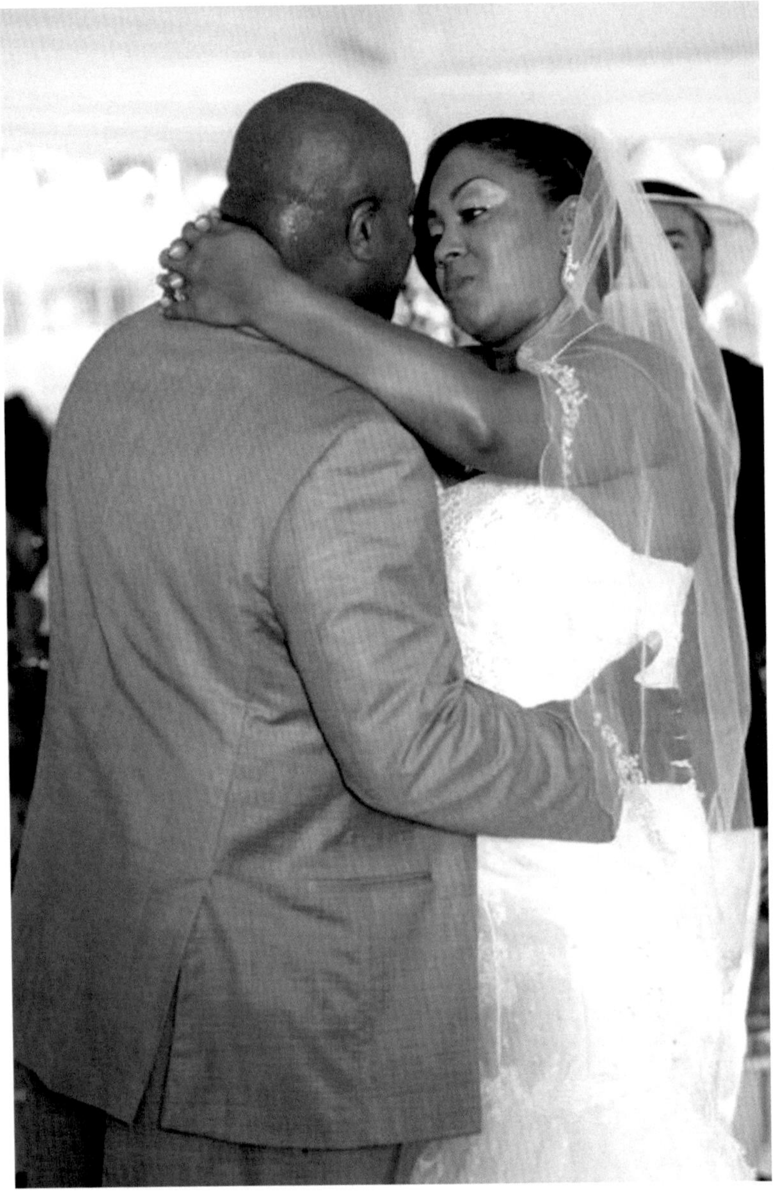

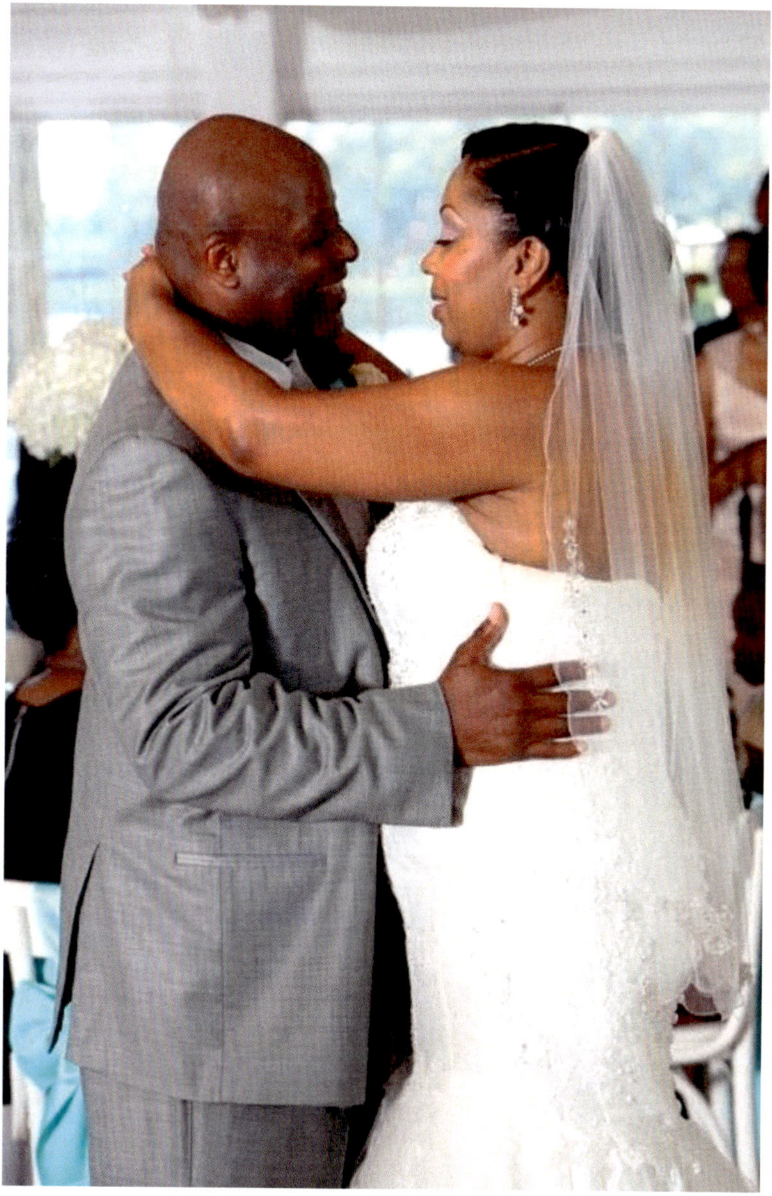

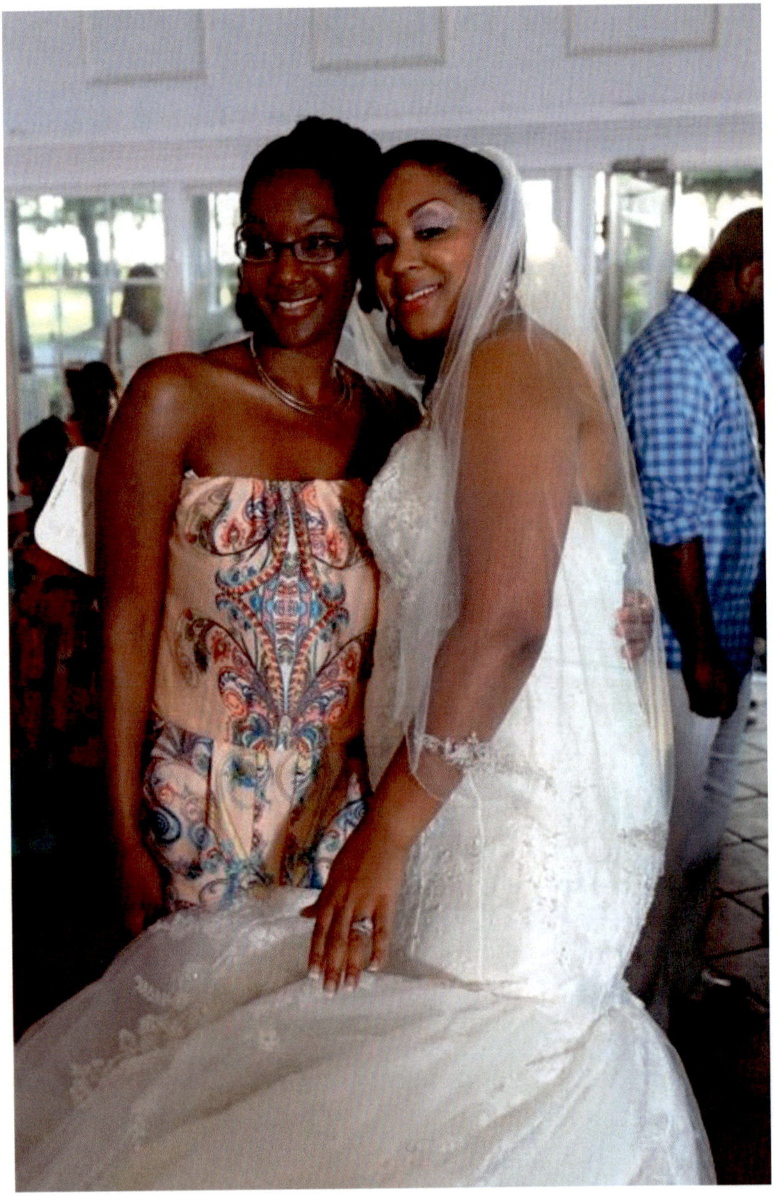

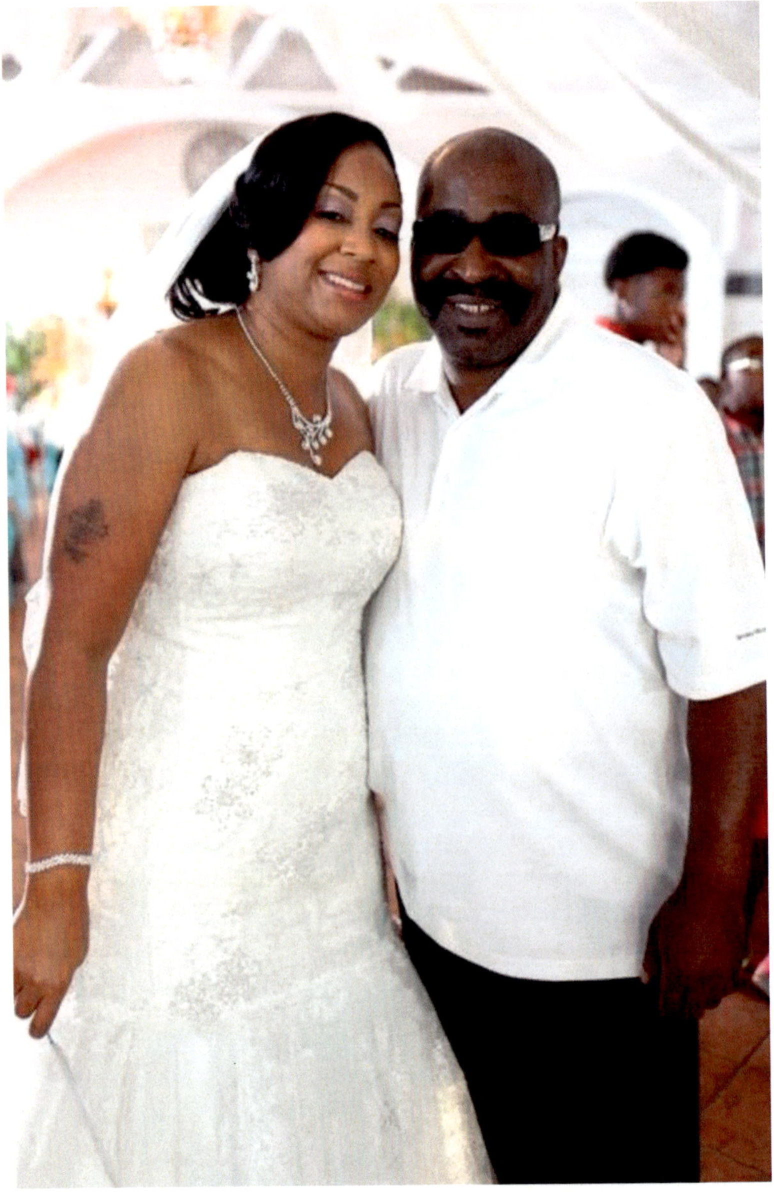

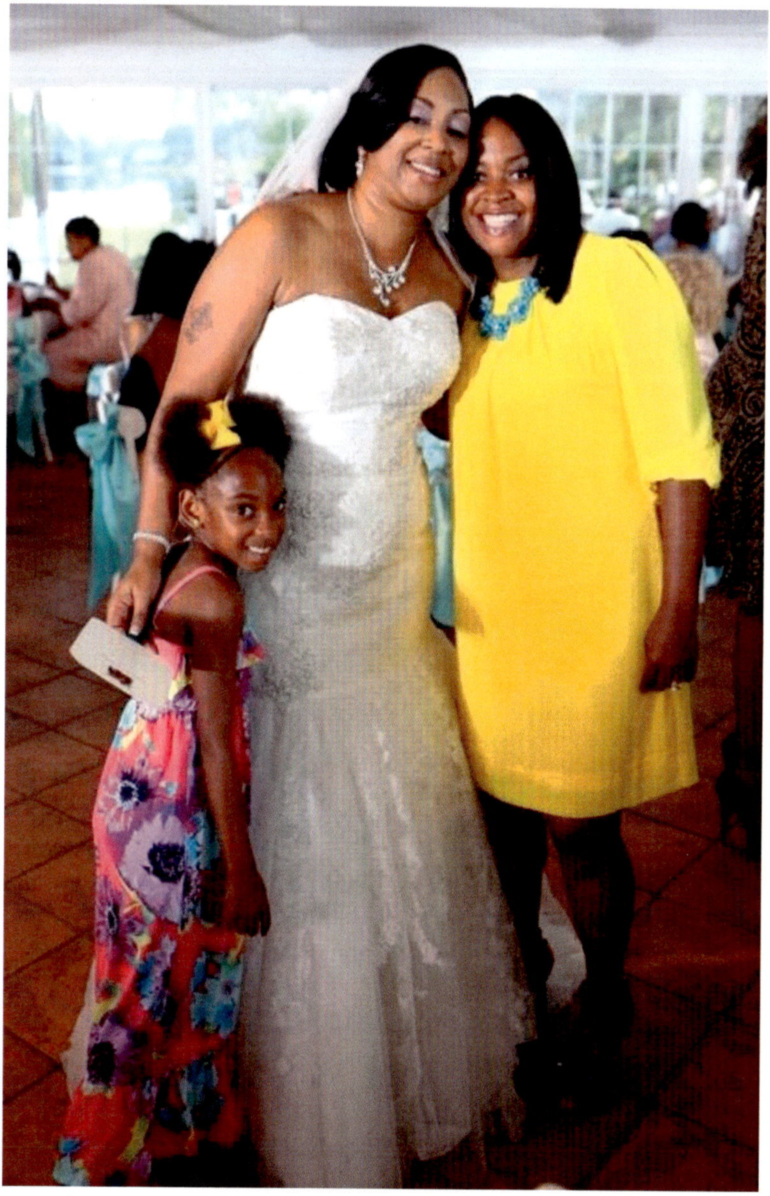

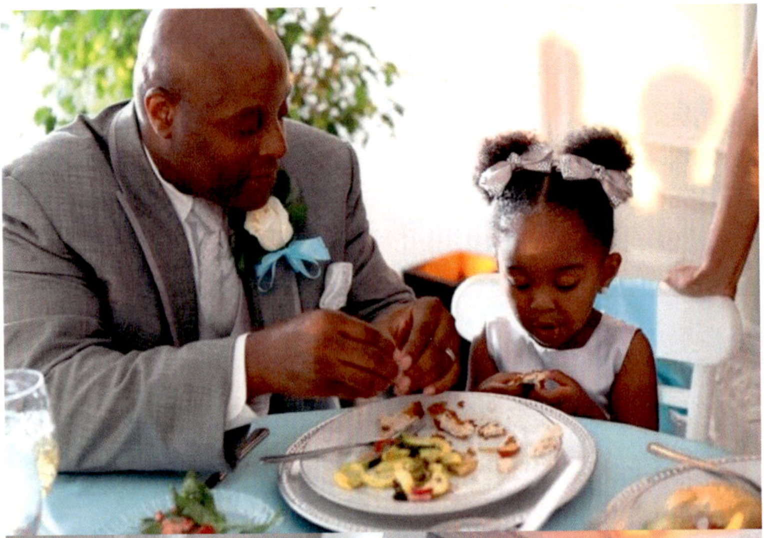

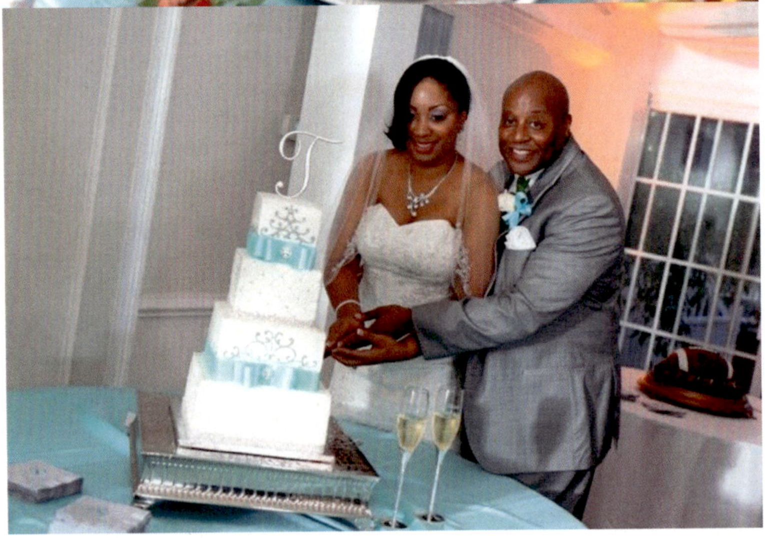

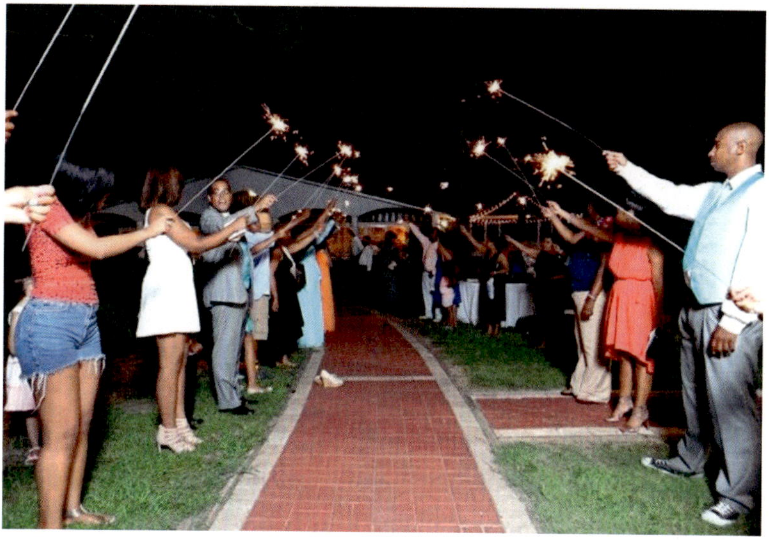

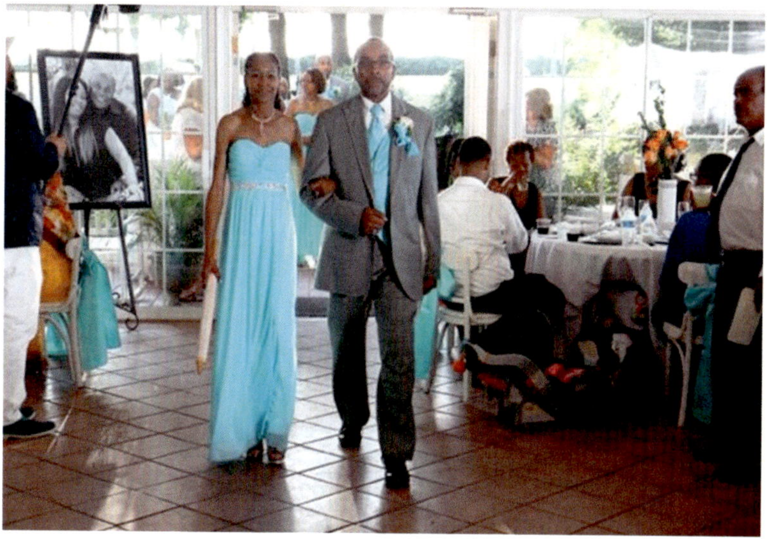

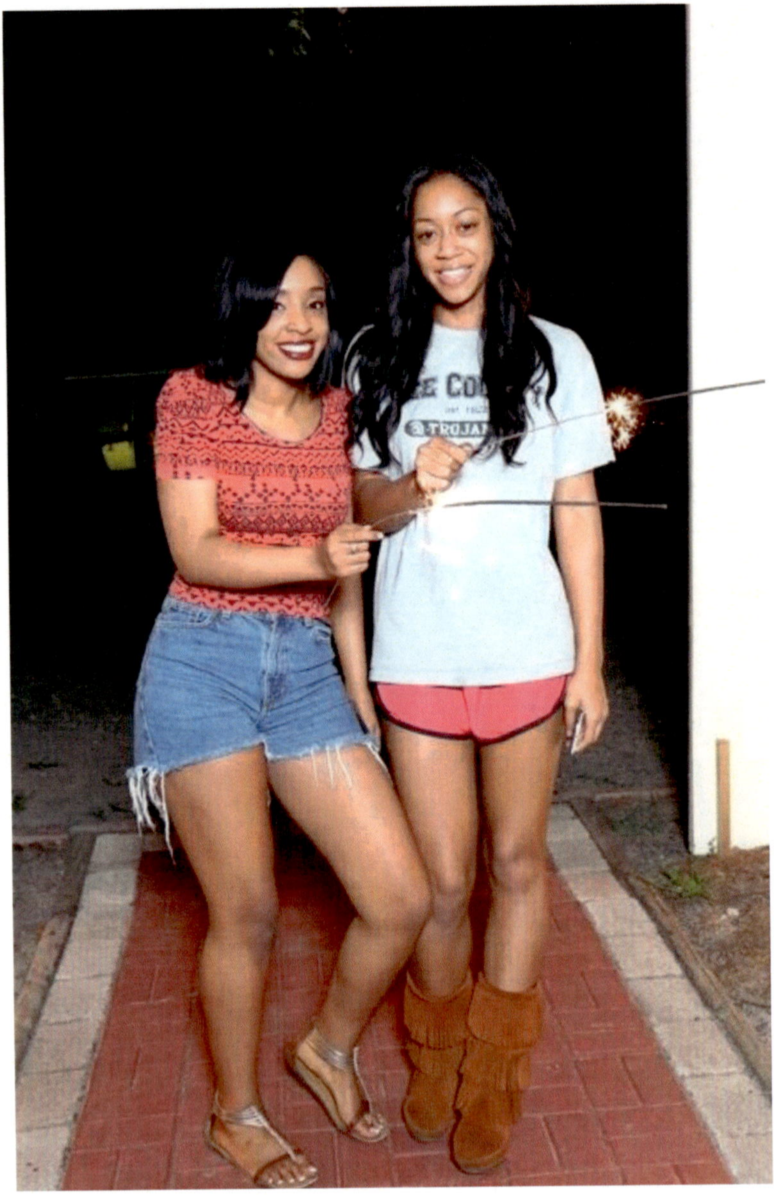

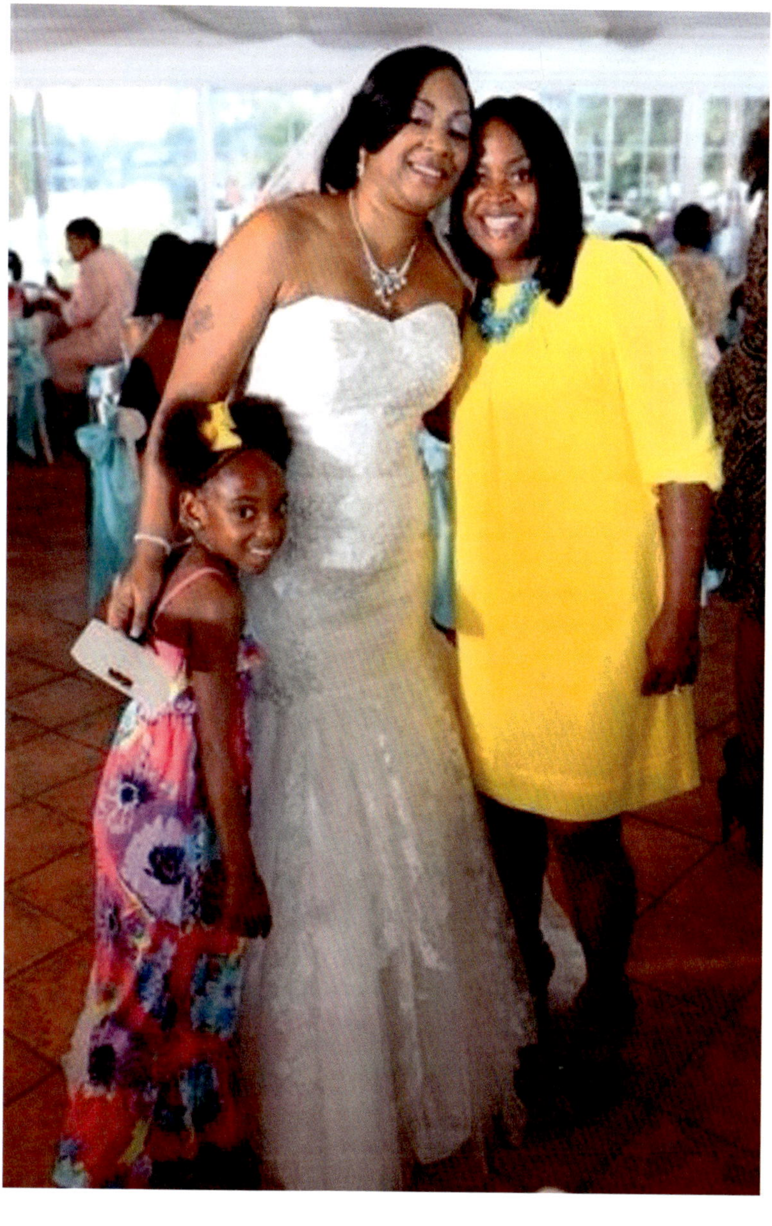

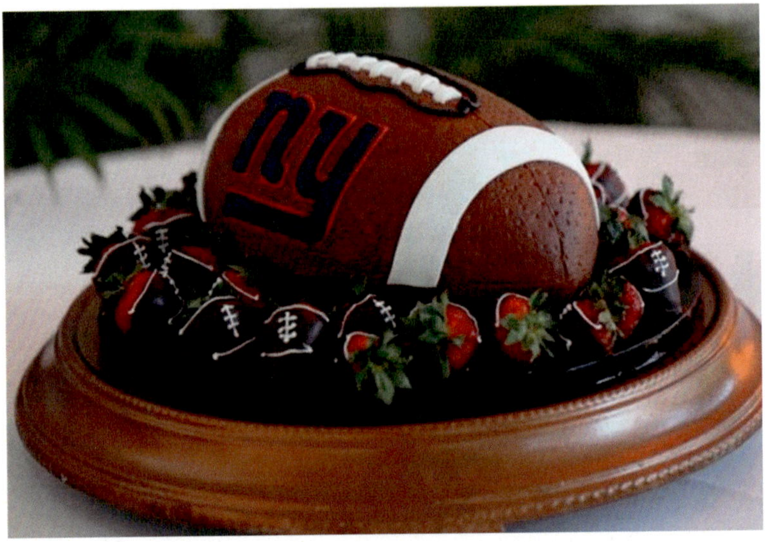

Made in the USA
Lexington, KY
17 January 2018